Music

Discover the Past, Present, and Future of Music Production, Technology, Techniques, Recording & Songwriting

Copyright Notice

No part of this book may be reproduced or transmitted in any form whatsoever, electronic, or mechanical, including photocopying, recording, or by any information storage or retrieval system without expressed written, dated and signed permission from the author. All copyrights are reserved.

Disclaimer

Reasonable care has been taken to ensure that the information presented in this book is accurate. However, the reader should understand that the information provided does not constitute legal, medical or professional advice of any kind.

No Liability: this product is supplied "as is" and without warranties. All warranties, express or implied, are hereby disclaimed. Use of this product constitutes acceptance of the "No Liability" policy. If you do not agree with this policy, you are not permitted to use or distribute this product.

We shall not be liable for any losses or damages whatsoever (including, without limitation, consequential loss or damage) directly or indirectly arising from the use of this product.

Discover How To Find Your Sound

Find Out More

Swindali music coaching/Skype lessons.

Email djswindali@gmail.com for info and pricing.

Table Of Contents

Introduction

Chapter 1. Music Stripped To The Core: Understanding Sound
    What Is Sound?
    Breaking Down The Sound Wave
    Manipulating Sound
    Types of Audio Signal

Chapter 2. The Evolution of Music Production
    Music Production In Brief
    The Changing Concept Of Music Producers

Chapter 3. The Music Producer
    Types of Music Producers

Chapter 4. The Music Production Blueprint
    Stages In Music Production
    Steps In Producing Music
        1. Writing the Song.
        2. Recording a Demo.
        3. Rehearsals.
        4. Recording basic tracks
        5. Overdubbing.
        6. Editing music
        7. Music Mixing
        8. Mastering

Chapter 5. Inventions and Insights That Changed Music
    Music Production VS Music Technology
    The Analogic Sound
    The Commercial Sound
    Difference Between Analog And Digital Sound Recording

Computers In Sound Recording
The Virtual Sound

Chapter 6. The Transformation of Music
The Record (1948)
The Compact Cassette Tape (1963)
8 Track Tape (1964)
The Floppy Disc (1972)
The Compact Disc (1982)
The MP3 (1992)
Streaming (2002)

Chapter 7. How Modern Technology Changed Music Production Forever
Effect Of Sound Reproduction
Aesthetic Approaches To Music Production
The Challenge Of Editing Takes And Mixing Tracks
The Changing Business World Of The Music Industry

Chapter 8. The Professional Art of Critical Listening
Balancing Objectivity and subjectivity
Why Listening Is Important To A Music Producer
Types of Listening
How To Listen Critically To Music

Chapter 9. The Most Important Skill For Music Producers
The Ways Of Listening

Chapter 10. Being a Music Producer
What a music producer needs

Chapter 11. Bringing Clarity To Music
The Importance of Genre
Defining genres
The evolution of popular music genres

Conclusion

Introduction

This book is about Music Production, how producing music evolved, its future directions, technologies, techniques, recording, and songwriting.

Music has been a central part of us humans and has been for thousands of years. It gives us a voice, the means with which to express our emotions. But like always, we change along with the changes that happen in our environment.

Of the changes we have experienced through time, the most significant occurring in recent decades is in technological advances, and this ever-evolving landscape of technology is reshaping every aspect of human activity; music is no exception. Such a shift has an impact not only the consumers but the practicing artists and experienced composers, as well.

What these changes mean and how these changes happen are issues that need to be understood especially by someone who wants to be a part of the music world. By understanding these shifts, practicing musicians and composers can make the most of the modern technology and incorporate these changes into their own works.

The change in music industry poses a challenge for music producers, recording studios, and the new and old musicians of today who may have to produce and record their music themselves.

Digital music is a new experience for most people of the 21st century. This easy-to-use technology has made making music possible to many aspiring musicians. The accessibility has made many people question the need for production experts and Audio engineers.

Producing and recording music is not as simple as many would think. An expert music producer can make or break a studio sound. For one who is not emotionally invested in the art, it may well be wise to learn and master the art and science of music production.

If you are one of those who aspire to be a music producer, you may need to learn music from across history, be able to point out genres, and know the past production techniques. Only by doing so will you be able to determine the different techniques of the past, reproduce them using today's technology, and incorporate them into your own work.

Read on and acquire the skills you need to produce and record music. Today's music climate is ripe for one who has the knowledge and skills for music production. Become a proficient music producer and stand out amongst the crowd.

Thanks for buying this book. I hope you enjoy it!

Chapter 1. Music Stripped To The Core: Understanding Sound

Whether your goal is to become a music producer or an audio engineer, understanding sound is basic to your chosen profession. It is through sound - the medium - that the art of music exists. And, technology is what bridges the sound and the music.

Making music is indeed fun, creative, and exciting. But, if you are to put music on record, you need to know the technical aspect of sound. It is fortunate that the science of sound is equally interesting. And, contrary to what one might think, learning the technical aspects of sound is not that difficult.

What Is Sound?

==Sound is the change in pressure of the air molecules and can exist in any medium, even under water.== To create sound, it is necessary to have an impetus to change the pressure in the air, like the string vibrations. *[impetus: the force that makes something happen or happen more quickly]*

Upon activating the stimulus, the air molecules that come into contact with the string, for example, become energized. The molecules that are in contact with the object, in turn, activate the molecules that are near resulting to a chain reaction. The activated molecules that are closest to our ear activate our ear drums and become the sound that we hear.

Breaking Down The Sound Wave

The chain reaction resulting from the changes in pressure of the air molecules create the sound wave, defined in three states – ==compression, rarefaction, and equilibrium.==

Compression is also referred to as "positive pressure." It is when the molecules are pushing on towards the next group of neighboring molecules. On the opposite side is the rarefaction where the molecules are moving away from their neighboring molecules, creating a vacuum. This is a "negative pressure" away from the neighboring molecules, referred to as a pulling force. Compression, therefore, is a pushing force and rarefaction the pulling force.

Equilibrium occurs when the amount of pushing force and the pulling force are equal resulting to a net force of zero.

The changes in the air molecules occur in a cycle:
- Air molecule (A) starts at the state of equilibrium
- When force is applied to air molecule (A) it starts to move towards its closest group of air molecules (B)
- With this movement from A to B, a vacuum begins to form behind air molecule (A)
- As air molecule (A) nears the next group of air molecules (B) positive pressure builds up and compression occurs
- When enough pressure builds up, air molecule (B) moves towards the next group of air molecule. When (B) moves away, a vacuum forms behind (A), the positive pressure decreases until the zero force is reached.
- Molecules (A) and (B) continue to move away from each other resulting to a vacuum. A state of rarefaction occurs where the vacuum expands creating more negative pressure until such state is reached where (A) and (B) starts moving towards each other leading to the next cycle.

- Note that the movement of (B) sets air molecule (C) into motion moving in the same cycle.
- This process is what makes the sound wave spread through the air.

It is interesting to note what happens with the interaction of sound waves. Imagine yourself pushing something with an amount of force (X). A friend decides to help and pushes with an amount of force (Y). The total amount of force used in pushing an object is (X) + (Y).

Translate this imaginary pushing into sound waves interacting with each other. If two sound waves push towards the same direction at the same time, the sum of both is your total amplitude.

Now, imagine holding a rope and pulling something with an (X) amount of force. Now, imagine further that a friend comes by and pulls the rope with a (Y) amount of force to the opposite direction. The total force applies is now (X) − (Y). Now, translate this scenario into sound. If one sound wave is in the compression state (the push) and another sound wave is in the state of rarefaction (the pull), the result is cancellation or what is referred to as a "null."

The property of sound waves and its functions are important for you to understand as it describes how complex sound forms. Then, you will learn how to manipulate sound waves.

Manipulating Sound

Sound technicians or engineers deal with both live sound and electrical sound, also known as audio signal. For instance, when you talk through a microphone, the voice converts into an audio signal. The audio signal possesses various properties and characteristics associated with all types of sounds that go through the sound system. Each sound source, like the microphone or a CD player, has separate channels on a mixing board, which must be balanced to create good sound which some experts in the music industry refer to as "joyful noise."

You can control and change the different audio signals or sounds by equalization and altering pitch, volume, and sound effects. Equalization is the process in which you modify sound frequencies to suit specific needs need. For example, the settings for equalization (EQ) for a musical format and a talk show are different. You can use equalizers to remove or minimize unwanted sounds such as unwelcome hums from amplifiers. In music production, equalization is used to adjust the tone quality of certain instruments or voices.

The quality of the sound you produce is determined by how you condition the sound through volume level mixing and equalization, as well as other settings that can be adjusted. Done the right way, the sound is good. The sound can end up bad or bland when the mix is done incorrectly. Other conditions may influence the sound to become bland including:

- Sound bounce. Sound can become bad when a second microphone picks up a voice and amplifies it after bouncing. The sound coming out of the speakers can sound bad. That's why in such a situation where there are several microphones in use, correct placement is necessary.
- Feedback. Feedback is another source of bad sound, and when it happens, it can cause awkward moments and frustrations. Feedback is that grating sound that you hear when a sound source, like a microphone, picks

up its own signal and then amplifies it from a speaker, resulting to a looping effect which can grow in volume and strength. Another source of this annoying sound is when the microphone is quite far from the sound source, causing you to increase the volume to try to compensate for the distance.

There are other things you need to avoid if you are to come up with music that sounds professional. These include (1) external noise coming from neighbors or rooms near your building, (2) computer noise that will likely affect the quality of your sound, like acoustical interference between computers and microphones, and computer fan, and (3) air conditioning noise. basically, COMPLETE SILENCE

On the other hand, what makes for a good sound comes from three parts: components that conditions the sound correctly for the unique environment, right placement of microphones to record the sounds, an expert technician who control and modify the sounds. If one of these parts is missing, your sound you create is not good.

Types of Audio Signal

Just as an artist chooses the medium to create a work of art – like the piano for a musician and oil on canvas for the visual artist, the sound engineer and technician need to choose the medium for the sonic masterpiece.

1. *Pressure Waves.* This is familiar to us since we hear them every day through our ears. An example is the tone "A" performed by a piano. When a musician presses the key of "A" on a piano, a felt-padded hammer strikes the appropriate string in the sound board. When

struck, the action triggers a vibration at a constant frequency, which in turn, is based on the string's length, thickness, and tension.

The vibrating string causes the air around it to move at the same frequency creating a chain reaction called pressure waves or sound waves. The constant frequency of key "A" is 440 Hz which the ear can receive and convert into electrical signals the brain can understand. This frequency in music is called pitch.

There are other factors that contribute to the sound produced, like timbre. Timbre is the essence of sound and what makes a specific sound different from others. What distinguishes the timbre is the material of the medium and its location. In the case of the piano or the guitar, its timbre is determined by the sound board, how dense the wood material is, and the room. Though both have the frequency of, for instance, 440 HZ producing the pitch "A", the quality of the sound produced are different.

2. *Electrical Audio.* A continuous stream of information represents this type of audio signal, which is also known as analog signal. An example is the speaker in your car which receives an electrical audio signal (*the input*) creating a vibration that results to the sound that you hear. The speakers would need a voltage to produce sound.

The same is true with a microphone. Microphones produce electric signals in proportion to the amount of sound the microphone receives. When the singing or voice stops, the information exists as electrons coursing through the cable. These electrons need to be changed into digital data to be received by a digital audio workstation.

3. *Digital Audio*. The digital audio is close to the electrical audio. It is represented by a pure voltage and is made of "1" and "0" with a level of threshold each. For instance, if the low threshold level is set at 0-2 volts and high at 4-6 volts, signal received that is below 2 volts will be defined as "0". If the signal received is above 4 but below level, it is to be defined as "1".

Analog and digital are two different language. But, the same message can be transmitted by different languages. But only those who speak the language can understand the message. In the case of the guitar (analog) communicating with the computer (digital), you would need a translator. In this case, you would need and analog to digital converter.

4. *MIDI Data*. MIDI data is different from the other types as it is a set of commands used to create sounds rather than representations of sound. MIDI is an acronym for Musical Instrument Digital Interface. Strictly speaking, MIDI is not music but can be used by a computer to create music. The digital binary information carries the date but, in itself, it is not sound.

Unlike live music where you cannot go back on a note sung out of tune, in MIDI data, you can fix a mistake by going back to where the error is and correct it. MIDI data is a list of parameters which allows you correct a mistake, change a pitch or tempo, or alter a whole musical passage. And, this is what makes the MIDI data great for recording purposes.

Chapter 2. The Evolution of Music Production

Working in the creative industries may prove to be difficult, considering the rapid changes in technology. To stay abreast of developments in the industry and be competitive, one has to keep pace with the changes and trend and know how these affect your work.

This is also true in music production since much of the technological advances transformed the way music is produced, how people listen, and how new and veteran musicians work.

If you plan to make music production as your career or intend to produce music on your own, being clear on the concepts of music production, music technology, and recording is the best way to start.

Music Production In Brief

There are several ways with which to describe music production. There are people who understand music production as a process, while others view it as a role requiring a multitude of skills.

As a process, music production goes through stages in sound production and recording. The whole process may include sessions with artists, coaching musicians, listening on recordings, providing suggestions for purposes of editing and alterations, scheduling record sessions and overseeing the recording and production of a single, track, or record. Music production may also involve collaboration with other professionals to ensure the record comes out well.

Through the years, music production has also been referred to as skills lumped together to mean a role. But, this term has evolved from its original meaning from fifteen years ago. Before the middle of the 1960s, the producer's role consists of being a fixer or someone who books artists, studios, and musicians.

Today, the role of a music producer has broadened to include the management of resources and time. The task of producing music varies from band to band, but the basic components remain the same. Music producers may write the materials themselves, but others may just want to oversee the production and ensure that the process is cohesive and productive of the desired result.

The Changing Concept Of Music Producers

Ask your friends or peers what a producer does, and you are sure to get differing answers. But, if you ponder deeper, the different answers tell you of the change in how music production is perceived today. Still, the answers highlight an important fact that there are two meanings to what a producer is.

Traces of the *bedroom production* were already evident during the 1900s, using hardware instruments. Its rise is due to the increase in computing power and the accessibility of inexpensive music technologies. A bedroom producer is usually a musician who produces music independently at home using electronic music. Unlike the traditional producer who oversees the whole recording process and works with a team, the bedroom producer creates music independently, from the creation of ideas, recording the music, and to releasing music. Often, these bedroom producers are self-taught, acquiring knowledge in sound design, music theory, and how to mix by online tutorials and reading blogs.

The so-called bedroom producers were successful and were considered true music producers in the historical sense. An example of a bedroom producer is Jahmaal Fyffe, known as Chipmunk, who at the age of 18 made his first album in a bedroom with a friend, assisted by an expert producer and an engineer. The album – *I am Chipmunk* – was released in 2009 and became a hit album, together with the singles "Oopsy Daisy" and "Diamond Rings."

Another famous bedroom producer is Jyoti Mishra who formed the White Town band in 1989. Mishra created his famous song *Your Woman* in his home in UK which became the no. 1 hit in 1997. A bedroom producer who made it to the New Artist Grammy Nomination in 2002 is David Gray. He made his fourth album *White Ladder* which included the singles *Babylon*. It was his music production of Babylon which catapulted Gray to fame.

The term bedroom producer may seem demeaning, but actually it is descriptive of a person who works at a sequencer in his home and produce music. Music production, in this sense, is making music sonically, unlike the making of music with the view of guiding creativity. *of or relating to sound*

Again, the concept of producer acquired a new meaning during the 1990s with the rise of the dance culture. The new meaning was attributed to the widespread use of new technology, such as the samplers, sequencers, and synthesizers which was communicated by MIDI. MIDI, an acronym for Musical

Instrument Digital Interface, is a language that lets musical instruments, computers, and other hardware communicate.

The significance of the music producer's perspective

While the professional focus of the music producer gives weight to their work, it is the application of their art that is more interesting. The studio or workstation is where the producer acquires new skills and sensitivities. It is a place where a producer continually learns and evolves.

It is the producer's perspective that will ultimately shape the type of producer one becomes. Whether the producer is the type who gets along well with people or one who uses technical expertise and creativity to enhance music, it is the perspective that guides the producer's development.

The producer then
Traditionally, the music producer is one who manages the project from studio personnel, musicians, finances, and the whole product. Music production meant managing the session, which may be contrary to what many believe a glamorous. The whole production process was restrictive, both financially and creatively.

In addition, there were other restrictions, such as the timeframe for rehearsals. A rehearsal is expected to last 3 hours at most. It was then the belief that rehearsals need not take more than three hours to be recorded. A pre-production should have been done before the rehearsal.

The producer today
Production today has different meanings, and encompasses a broader range of activities. Music genres have become diverse

and seem to set aside the traditional model. Before, a producer is the producer, distinct from the artist who can be both writer and performer. Today, artists can become co-producers, and it is possible for producers to take part in songwriting and performance.

Further, with the appearance of the latest dance genres, like house and trance music, the concept of producer could mean the combined role of writer and producer. And, it is even more interesting to note that in the house and trance model, music is produced alone with no other human assistance, except perhaps a solo session vocalist.

Many may not be aware of the fact that many compositions for the dance music genre, like the trance, demands skill and effort, much like the traditional songwriting. Traditionally, a song is written with an acoustic guitar, later to be developed as a complete song.

In trance, the complex technique used to produce a song may not be appropriate on an acoustic guitar. Further, the production and composition goes hand in hand in a trance. Which goes to say that there are some music that cannot exist without the assistance of technology. This leads to the blurring of the term producer from its traditional benchmark.

The easy access of technology has reduced the necessity of a producer in the traditional sense. One can make music sound good before actually composing anything with substance. The process has been reversed such that where composing comes first and making it sound good later, now, one comes up with something that sounds good and fill it with the composition after. Imaging buying an expensive and beautiful frame first and paint an exquisite image after.

As we can see, the production role remains constant, but the pressures are different. Not only did pressures increase, the producer's lifestyle has also undergone changes. Where in the past, a producer belongs to a label or work in a recording studio, today the producer's role depends on being a freelance. A producer today has to work hard to be in business, working long hours, and with great personal responsibility.

The Current Climate
The music industry now may be highly competitive, financial-wise, but despite this environment, more music is available today than before. The driving force in the increase in music today is the accessibility of music production tools in the past few years. If one has a home computer and equipped with the know-how, it is possible to develop a high, studio-quality music production without the time and budget limitations of the music production in the past.

The effect of this change in the music industry is evident in the way artists are nurtured, in the producers' lifestyle, and in the music industry's revenue.
Whereas in the past, artist development was given much importance, the financial squeeze reduced this aspect in music production. Further, the excessive lifestyle within the pop and rock scenes in the '70s and '80s also ended. Another is the decrease in record companies' sale of products due to digital downloads and copying.

On the other hand, the change in climate within the music industry led to new types of signing. And, this has also led to the appearance of new genres, which though small in terms of clientele and sales, was able to hold on to a solid following for years.

The diverse changes in the current climate offer aspiring producers and musicians the opportunities for their music to be heard. It is now possible for music to have a professional presence even without a contract or for careers in the music industry to continue without the services of big labels.

An example of a new method was one used by *Marillon*, a band in UK. They sent emails to their fan base asking if they are willing to pay for an album up-front. This method was successful, and made it possible for them to write and produce <u>*Anoraknophobia*</u>. Another method of music production which appeared is the DIY, as exemplified by songwriter and folk musician Seth Lakeman.

Chapter 3. The Music Producer

The early concept of a music producer's role is best exemplified by the works of Sir George Martin, considered as the icon for the early model. He was an English music producer, composer, arranger, conductor, musician, and audio engineer. Martin was known as "The Fifth Beatle" due to his broad involvement with the Beatles' original albums.

Already a success even before getting involved with the Beatles, Martin nurtured and developed the musical and creative forces within the Beatles. His work with the Beatles included writing and arranging the string parts, and in the technical processes required in creating the sounds. Martin's work with the Beatles became a new perspective which was long-lasting.

Martin's style, however, is no longer applicable today. Music production and a producer's role now are understood in many different ways. Though still followed by some pop and rock genres today, Martin's way of producing music is viewed as "traditional."

Traditionally, music production encompassed the work of overseeing the process, guiding the people, nurturing the talent, and enhancing the music. Here, the producer's role is to guide the artist to a level where the music is realized. One may say the traditional role allows the music producer *creative control* of a production process. Realization of the music may take the form of releasing the created music for commercial purposes. Or, it may take the form of an artistic realization where the driving force is to come up with something innovative and creative, regardless if the music sells or not.

Whatever form the role may take in producing music, the producer's role is crucial. To view making music as just a creative role in the recording process is misleading. There are more important aspects to a producer's work that may be less influential and fun, but as important to its creative counterpart.

Types of Music Producers

A music producer's creations can take many forms. It may take the form of closely overseeing musicians in a rehearsal room, preparing music for tracking, to keeping close to the technical approach of production. These forms can be classified into two broad types: musician producer and engineer producer.
Trevor Horn exemplifies the musician producer, while Hugh Padgham provides the best example for engineer producer.

Hugh Padghan is an audio engineer and record producer. Padgham's entry into record production was influenced by Elton John's *Tumbleweed Connection*. He started as a tape operator and worked his way to becoming an audio engineer, working with artists such as Genesis, Police, and Phil Collins.

Padgham is known for his "gated drum" sound used by Phil Collins in his single <u>*In the Air Tonight.*</u> The "gated drum" sound is achieved by having a densely compressed room ambiance added to the original sound. This audio effect became popular and used a template for recorded pop drum sound of the 1980s.

Where Padgham focused on audio engineering, Trevor Horn spent time on the musical development of the artists. He left the sound engineering aspect on experts and subcontracted projects to trusted friends he had worked with for years.

Whether one is a musician producer or engineer producer depends on the skills possessed and learned on the job. A producer may either develop a strong musicality or acquire engineering skills and knowledge. The inclination to one or the other would depend on the quality focus the producer exerts.

Today, however, the concept of music producer has taken many forms. If you ask music producers today, you will get different answers depending on the dominant attention given by each to their work. These can be categorized into six types.

1. *Engineer producer.* The engineer is the most common view of a producer. This type is hands-on, works bent over the soundboard and obsessed with compression settings, reverb tails, and equalization. The engineer producer possesses a solid foundation of the technical side of recording music. This type could have been an engineer before entering music production and rose up the ranks to become a producer.

2. *The mentor producer.* This type may have been a recording artist before becoming a producer. As such, this type knows what the artists need. Knowing what artists are, the mentor producer knows how to coach, motivate, and encourage them to perform at their best. Because of the background experience of the mentor producer, they seem to be gifted with fresh insights and can refocus artists of their core strengths.

An example of this type of producer is Rick Rubin. He selects the engineers to handle the technical side of production, while he focus his work with the artist and realize his intent.

3. *The Golden Ticket producer.* This type of producer has a proven track record and can guarantee success for artists who work with this type. The success of this type could be because of his networking abilities, ability to collaborate with other professionals in the industry, knowledge of the trends in music and in technology, and in managing the studio. This type of producer brings about success and shares this success with recording artists.

An example of this type of producer is Dr. Dre who seems to hold magic for anyone who works with him. He is in-sync with the music industry and seems to have an eye for what's trendy but he does not forget his hip-hop roots.

4. *The remixer.* The concept of remix is to transform an existing track into a new one. The alteration could be anything, from a simple sonic change already existing in the mix, adjustments in structure or arrangement, or creative reworking of the original song's aesthetics. The one characteristic of remix is that it changes other materials to come up with a new one.

Remixing has existed since the late 19th century when new technologies made it possible for people to rearrange the listening experience. With the introduction of multitrack recording, the alterations became popular.

Modern remixing can be traced back to Jamaica's dance hall culture in the late 1960s to early 1970s. This dance culture was adapted by local music mixers who changed the tracks to suit the taste of audiences. Engineers and producers, like Lee "Scratch" Perry, popularized the stripped-down versions of reggae tunes. One figure of note for is Tom Moulton who popularized the dance remix known today.

Simultaneous with the 1970s disco, the dub and disco remix meld with the Jamaican immigrants in the Bronx and created what became known as the hip-hop music. Perry and Grandmaster Flash pioneered the use scratching and cutting and became part of the dance culture.

5. *The Musician.* This type is first a musician before becoming a producer. The musician-producer is much involved with recording tracks for their artists. The role may involve playing an instrument while orchestrating the whole process of tracking.

Trevor Horn is an example of a musician-producer who earned the name "The Man Who Invented the Eighties" due to his influence on pop music during this time.

6. *The Artist.* This type is an artist who takes full control of the album and is the producer at the same time. This artist is backed with successes, coupled with considerable experiences in the producing and recording technologies.

From the type of producers above, we can see that each has different role focus, depending on the skills possessed and background experience. If you are an aspiring music producer, it is not necessary for you to be schooled in music or acquire engineering training to be successful as a producer. You can start from where you are, the skills that you have, and gain the needed experience. This may take time, but the success you get later is worth it.

Chapter 4. The Music Production Blueprint

Though many artists today write and produce music in a smaller studio, much of the production occurs in an integral and iterative way. This method of producing music is easy due to the tools existing today and to the nonlinear way of editing. In whatever method, though, planning is still critical in the making of music.

Before going on to the process of music production, it is best to be clear with the term "production." When one refers to music production, it could mean the process of expressing the creativity and artistic development of music, whether production is done in or out of the studio. Another view for production is the process itself. Here, production refers to the technical aspect of producing a product, like the CD.

Stages In Music Production

Any product published goes through a production process. Initially, the process may have undergone a trial and error experience. From this experience, it may have been refined, which created and defined the systems and procedures relied upon today.

Russell Hepworth-Sawyer and Craig Golding (2011) identified seven stages in music production: inception, composition, pre-production, capture and forming, post production, production, and marketing and distribution.

Inception refers to having an idea and allowing it to flourish. The idea may come from an experience or from other sources of inspiration. There could be many ideas that crop up, some will be shed, but one is sure to reach the drawing board.

Composition may not be an option for some producers as they can hire artists to do this work for them. However, in the current climate and in so many methods available for dealing, producers need to protect their revenue streams. Therefore, many of the producers with insight start to engage in the writing process.

Pre-Production refers to the preparation done with the purpose of improving productivity all throughout the process. Since the objective is to earn an income, the business side of production needs to be considered. Questions a novice or seasoned producer could ask are: Is the project feasible? How to start the project? Who are the people the project would need? Answers to these questions will guide the remaining steps of the process.

Capture and forming is where the producer creates the structure and arrangement of the music. In music production, this is called mixing to create a balance in the sounds produced.

Postproduction is that stage where the music is prepared for the medium for mass production. It is also at this stage where music is improved and balanced.

Production refers to the means with which the material is collated and reproduced. This part may be of the least interest to the artist, but this should be given of equal interest. Reproduced material should maintain as much quality as possible to be accepted in the market.

Steps In Producing Music

In creating something, whether it be in art or in any discipline, you start with a fundamental building block. The building blocks should be tried and tested and proven to work consistently. In music production, these blocks become your basis for making decisions for moving forward to the next step in the process. Further, when you encounter a challenge, the foundation blocks help you come up with intelligent decisions that would lead to your desired result.

1. Writing the Song.

Songwriting starts with an idea you have or an inspiration. The idea may come from a melody or a lyric. Or it may come from a chord progression, an improvisation, or a unique sound. Once you have the idea developed, the process of music production starts.

The modern songwriting method is different from the traditional way of doing it. Traditionally, a song is written with an instrument for the melody or words for the lyrics. If you follow the traditional way of writing a song, the band members would likely get bored and restless while you experiment with the lyrics and the melody. However, if you prefer to write in the traditional way, it is best to write alone or with somebody who can help you assess your idea.

The songwriting today has many resources to draw on and may not need a band to work on in producing music. Working on a template removes the necessity of having a band play a part repeatedly. Examples of modern resources are samples and music loops in the flow of ideas and set the background for writing an inspired song.

<u>Principles of writing a song</u>

- Subject matter

This is what your song is about. The subject matter lays the foundation for the decisions you make in music production. For instance, if you are writing about drug addiction, the music elements you choose should be oppressive and dark to support your message, which could be that of helplessness or depression. But, the dark mood will not be appropriate if you are writing dance music.

- Telling the story

This principle is about how you convey your message. For example, you can use a minor key when telling a sad song or a major key when you are talking about a happy moment. The relationship between lyric and melody must be supportive of each, otherwise, your listener gets confused and the song sounds "off."

The relationship between lyric and melody is crucial and no amount of technical solutions can help resolve an issue, should there be one.

A plugin or a compressor will not be of any help in changing the feeling of the song. The technical tools serve to enhance the music's energy present in the song. This is why the songwriting process should be right before going into the music production process.

- Capturing the listeners' attention

If you are writing the song, you need to decide how you are going to present it. Shall you use the dynamic energy or should you go simple at the start and end dramatically? Or would you rather start big, drop, and go high again at the end?

This principle deals with the structure of the song. The classic example starts with a verse, followed by a chorus, and a repeat back and forth of the two. This can be broken by the bridge sections, giving you another perspective of the song.

You can capture the interest of your audience if you are creative in writing your song and in using the sounds to support the lyrics through imagery. For instance, the repetitive sound production could represent the drab and monotonous pattern of everyday living.

If the production of music is done properly, the imagery can evoke memories in a person and relive these memories through your music.

- Bring out feeling

A well written song will suggest the dynamic changes of your story. The story in your song will tell you when to fade out or go with a bang. Without the dynamic changes, the song sounds bland and your listener gets bored.

You get to know if your song is ready for music production if you feel the music. That is to say, you stop thinking and just feel your music. Observe yourself if there are sections where you get distracted and lose interest. Remember that in music, feeling outweighs thinking. If you are trying to convince a person about how good your song is, then something must be wrong.

On a final note, avoid asking somebody for an opinion about your song, unless that somebody is an expert or a professional producer. A friend will tell you what you want to hear, and therefore, not an objective assessment of the song.

2. Recording a Demo.

Recording can be as simple as recording a single instrument with voice or a mock recording that demonstrates what the track sounds like after recording. Whatever your purpose for recording, it should convey the message of the song, since this will be used as reference for all those who are involved in the production of the project.

Demo recording is often made a part of the recording process. When ideas crop up, these are captured piecemeal and put together to create a song. Demo recording may not be coherent, but once the issues are worked out, this is re-recorded as a single performance. Demo recording is useful as this method allows you to discover issues that you can solve before going into the real recording studio.

Another critical benefit of demo recording is the development of music production elements and the song. It enables you to test ideas without necessarily perfecting them. For example, it is not necessary for a harmony added to a song section to be in time or in tune. You just need to know if the harmony brings out the emotion intended in the song or the effect you envision.

In sum, demo recording is great for generating ideas. It is a great means of determining what works and what does not work before you commit it to the final production process. Or, you might find out that your record demo is fit to become the final product. An example is the Jagged Little Pill of Alanis Morissette. The demo vocals that was so full of emotion and power was difficult to reproduce and was decided to be used on the final production.

In demo recording, you can use any of these three approaches:

    a.   *Using the band.* An advantage of using the band is the opportunity of getting the input of others who think as you do. Since band members specialize in their respective instruments, they can assist you in creating parts that are not typical. Musicians, especially if they are good, are sensitive to the sound and can adjust their performance to sync with the other performers.

Note, however, that not all musicians have sensitivities. They can break your song if they are not sensitive to the nuances of the music. You, therefore, need to communicate your intention clearly, tell them of the song's message, feeling, and its motivation.

Another thing you should be aware of is that in working with different personalities, conflict is unavoidable. If possible, work with people who think like you or who compliments your personality. This way, you will have less conflict during work and you can complete the project smoothly.

    b.   *Do-it-yourself record demo.*

Today's technology offers access to any form of instrument that can help you in your creative work. It can be through a MIDI, a pre-recorded music, or a raw sample of a part that you can perform yourself. There is a library of sound and the technologies available that can aid you achieve your vision in demo recording.

The advantage of doing a demo recording yourself is that you are in full control of the process. You can achieve the best results through this method if you are clear with what you want, and have the ability to program or perform it. It may sound easy, but the difficulty is in being honest with yourself when listening to your music.

When recording demo yourself, your biggest obstacle is honesty. You need to be honest with yourself about what works and what part needs to be discarded. It is easy to convince yourself that your work is good, especially if there is no one who can listen objectively to your music. If this is the case, you might be limiting your song potential or, at most, destroying it.

Artists who produce on their own succeed because they have the guidance or assistance of a producer. Other artists collaborate with songwriters or listen to the opinion of people they respect. You need people who can point out to you honestly and objectively what is wrong with your song.

    c. *Getting production help.* There will be times when you are deep into the details of the work that you lose sight of the overall vision of the song and your perspective. This is a common issue among artists who focus more on the production elements before the essentials of the song are written and established. In such case, it is a signal to get help and to have a new perspective.

There is nothing wrong with seeking the help of trusted others. By inviting someone in, you the benefit of fresh listening who may detect issues in the song and suggest a new direction when recording your demo. Another benefit you get is detecting problem areas which may not have been apparent to you before. Keep in mind that when you do seek help, be open and seriously work with the person.

3. Rehearsals.

Rehearsals are often viewed as live performances, but they should be considered as important to the production process. Rehearsals are all about making sure that everybody in the band knows what they are doing, and how to do it. Part arrangements and issues on sounds can easily be addressed in rehearsals and with less pressure.

Other than band rehearsals, it is also necessary to rehearse when working with hired musicians or vocalists who may not be familiar with your song. It is safer to assume the possibility of unforeseen issues than be sorry later. This way, the artist is better prepared to deal with the environment at the recording studio.

> The list below gives you an idea of matters the band rehearsals can resolve:
>
> - Learning song arrangement
> - Establishing the bpm and to note it
> - Focusing on individual parts and how the different instruments fuse together
> - Determining the best instrument and tone for each part

- Discovering and resolving issues that may not have been apparent during demo recording
- Getting rid of musicians who do not have the appropriate feel for the part
- Identifying additional resources needed for the coming recording

Tips for efficient band rehearsals:

- Send demo recording before rehearsal sessions. This is easy if you convert your demo recording into an mp3 file and send it through email. Make sure each band member receives the demo and have listened to them before the rehearsal session. You may skip this if the band members are already familiar with the song.

- Organize and schedule band rehearsals. When working with a group of musicians, decide who needs to be present for the basics of the rehearsal. For example, you don't need the background singers to be present if you are working on the arrangement with the section on rhythm.

- Consult with the studio engineer. When you are done rehearsing the parts and sections of the band, bring in the studio engineer who will do the recording. The studio engineer can suggest sounds, what resources that are available in the studio, and what to expect during the session.

4. Recording basic tracks

In recording basic tracks, you can take either of two ways: the professional tracking session or in a home environment session. The determining factor in choosing the basic track recording is your budget.

The Professional tracking session

Booking a professional recording studio does not necessarily mean that everything will go smoothly as planned. When you have decided on a recording studio, visit it and take note of the following:

- The size of the live room. How big is it?
- Talk and observe your voice for any weird tonal changes
- Can you get the sense of the room's tone when you hit a kick or snare drum?
- Are there any isolation booths? How many?
- Check of a good sight line between musicians from the booth to control room to live room
- Is there a good stock of amps for bass and guitar and are they in good condition?
- Check the microphones in the list against those actually in the studio
- Is the facility shared with another studio? Is there no conflict in the availability of your time booked?
- Does the price quoted include an engineer?
- Is an assistant engineer available?
- Is there a condition if you go over time?
- Can you get your gear into the studio the night before the session?

If the information you need to know is overwhelming for you, hire a professional engineer who can help find a recording place that is suitable to your needs. An experienced professional engineer can detect problems in a recording place and can give valuable advice that can save you money, time, and unnecessary inconveniences.

Do not just rely on the word of a manager or a studio owner when booking a recording place. In a highly competitive market, they would do what it takes to get you to use their facilities. Once you book, you are on your own when making the basic tracks with the equipment that is available in the studio.

The home studio recording

A home studio environment can prove to be difficult when recording basic track than in a commercial facility. But, it does not necessarily mean you cannot come up with a good basic track or even better. What you do need to achieve your purpose is to plan carefully.

- Careful placement of instruments. Recording in a home studio means smaller space to work in. This can be even more complicated if a drum kit is involved.

The best way is to use the kick drum as a reference point for your drum sound. The reason is that the kick is affected by the resonance in the room which size is smaller than 20 x 20 feet. Position your kick drum at the center of the room, and then try to move around the room while facing the instrument. This you, you can make sure that the drummer and his entire drum kit can fit in the setting.

Test the kick drum by hitting it until you find the sweet spot where the sound is strongest but is not over resonant where there is too much ringing or vibration, or too muddy where the lower mids feel cluttered and the bottom end of the sound is not clear enough.

The purpose is to find the best placement that produces the right resonance when striking the drum shell. When done, get the rest of the drum kit set up around this placement. Use the same method when setting up the other instruments.

When capturing sounds for your basic track, let your ears be the judge for what is good and what is not.

- Use of Gobos. These refer to go-betweens which are reflective barriers set between instruments, hence the name. They serve in tightening or controlling the room's resonances or reverb to affect the sound that goes into the close mikes. As a general rule, it's best that the drum kit is surrounded by a semicircular wall from the back end. However, such a shape is uncommon. In any case, just make sure that there are no gobos that obstruct sound at the front of the drum kit.

The idea behind the use of the gobos is reduce early reflections in the mike that can adversely flatten or color the sound of the drums. Check that the distance of the drum kit to a surface except the floor is not closer than 10 feet or you will have a problem with the sound. Early reflections cause an effect called comb filtering which results to a muddy, indistinct, undefined, or thin sound. In a home studio environment, the use of mattresses, packing blankets, or couch cushions can help suppress the negative effects.

Using gobos when recording multiple instruments is also great to isolate the bleeds between instruments and give you control of each sound in the mix.

- Miking techniques.

The truth is, microphone techniques are the foundation of any recording endeavor. In the industry, miking techniques refer to the kind of microphone utilized and more importantly, mic placement.

These two are key in producing polished tone. You'll see that when you record sound with good microphones and mic placement, it's so much easier to process and mix the tracks compared to doing the same to tracks that have been recorded without considering placement or quality.

If you're new to music production, you'll realize fairly soon that there are so many kinds of tones that become available to you by just manipulating mic placement. Even the smallest changes in position can help you get exactly the kind of sound you're hoping to get for your music.

You can use any of the following techniques.

Spot miking – This entails placing the mic near the sound source, typically within a foot or two. This is often used in home recording because it minimizes the amount of reverb (which is the sound of the room) that is added to the recorded sound.

Stereo Miking – This refers to the practice of using two microphones in order to capture the stereo field on an instrument. However, modern technology has developed to stereo mics that could be utilized on their own to capture an entire stereo field. A variety of this kind of miking exists including Spaced Pair, which is typically used for acoustic guitar tracking, in which two small condenser mics are placed 2 and a half feet from each other, with one being placed to capture overall tones and one meant to capture the small details.

Distant miking - This involves placing a mic about 3 or 4 feet from the sound source, allowing to capture some of the sounds of the room in addition to the instrument. An example of this kind of mixing is overhead miking. This is usually the case with drum kits in which two or more mics are used – one is placed approximately 32 inches over the snare directly pointing down, while one is typically placed above the drummer's right shoulder, pointing toward the snare. The configuration has many variations.

Combined miking techniques – You'll likely have to use more than one placement technique especially as you start to experiment with different kinds of music and genre.

You can use as few as 3 mikes or go ham and get more, but there's a golden rule in miking: you need to know what to keep your eyes on. Keep in mind that placement is usually dictated by the musical genre as well. Don't worry because there is a guide at the last chapter of this book that should give you a crash course on the different genres. However, the way to learn these about genres is through listening to music.

The kind of sound or equipment you need to record is also a factor. In recording drum sounds for example, professional producers have their own preferences but there's one thing that many of them agree on: overhead mikes are crucial. Make these your priority, Kick mic will be next, and snare mic last.

The purpose of an overhead mic is to capture the drum sound's essence for the basic track. This represents the drum kit's real stereo perspective. The overhead mikes can also capture your cymbals' sounds, and room's kick and snare sound.

Recording vocals is another matter. Lead vocals in particular are one of the most important parts of the music production. They convey the narrative of the lyrics and the soul of the music (or the artist) while carrying the melody. Some music producers prefer the Single Large Diaphragm Condenser setup in which a very sensitive microphone is used, picking up the vocals and the sound of acoustic guitar resulting to a thick sound where the instrument is quite prominent. Some use a stereo setting to create crisp sound signals.

You can experiment with the different mikes. That should help you identify what works best given your recording space.

Be careful, though, with the number of mikes you use. If you use more mikes, it will be more difficult to capture good sound.

- Capturing sounds and level adjusting. Ensure that you allocate a lot of space when you set up the basic tracks levels. The reason for this alert is the insufficient power supplies and inexpensive components. Note that performers play louder during recorded a performance as opposed to just capturing sounds. Set the levels to 3-6 dBFS less than the sound you really want to produce.

Further, make sure that the musicians are playing their parts at the right tempo before you set the sounds. This oversight is common among new engineers who are capturing basic tracks. For instance, let's say the sound is set at 90 bpm while the drummer plays at a range of 125 bpm, this will result to tighten the sounds, which will improperly affect the sound of the drum.

Since sound is different for each song, you'll have to make the necessary modifications for every track. One method that works is to record together songs that are alike in vibe and tempo to minimize adjustments. Another tip that works is to adjust the drum room's acoustics to compensate the tempo. A rule to remember is: if the tempo is quick, the room must be less reverberant.

You will encounter a lot of issues in basic track recording. When you do, let your ears be the judge and do not hesitate to start over when you think something is wrong. When everything that you do just does not work, then just do it again using a different approach. Starting over is a lot better than wasting time and effort. On the plus side, you would have learned new ways of recording.

5. Overdubbing.

Overdubbing is a technique used to add musical parts on a pre-existing track and performs along with it. The purpose of overdubbing could be creative in nature. Or, the reason is to fix a mistake in a previous recording. Overdubbing became popular among musicians with the appearance of multitrack recording.

You can correct mistakes on any musical part which occurred in the original performance. The mistake can be on the drums, vocals, guitars, or any other instrument. You can re-record the part until you are satisfied it is performed right.

You have to remember, however, that for overdubbing to be successful, match the re-recorded parts sonically with the original performance. That is to say, use the same guitar, microphone, amplifier, same set up, and preferably, overdub during the same session.

However, it may not always possible to overdub during the session or on the same day. Mistakes may have been noticed when re-recording another part. When this happens, replicate the set up used when recording the original performance. Otherwise, you will have to re-record the part for the tracks to match.

This is why you need to take note of the exact placement of equipment used. If you are an engineer, it is advisable to write down or take pictures of everything used in recording an instrument. This may take time, but it is a proven good practice.

You learned in chapter 1 of this book that sound is a wave. One hertz (Hz) is one cycle per second. Therefore, 20 Hz sound wave is made of up 20 cycles per second. When you are using multiple microphones or speakers, and if you want to capture or reproduce a sound source, make sure that the sound captured is at exact points of its cycle. If not, you are going to have phase issues where sound waves are not aligned with each other. This will result to a loss of specific frequency. When you see two points located 180 degrees opposite of each other, you get what is called as phase cancellation. Phase cancellation is where sound waves are "out of phase", resulting to lost or weakened frequencies.

For example, you are recording a guitar amp using two microphones. You have to place microphones in such a way that it aligns with the cycle of the sound sourced from the amp. You can do this by moving the mike back and forth and listening to it until you are sure they align.

How to do overdubbing
If you are new to overdubbing, here is an example to give you an idea how overdubbing is done. Let us suppose you have a band coming in to record a track:

1. The drummer record with the click track.
2. The guitarist plugs into a direct input (DI) box. The guitarist serves to guide the drummer as to how the song is played.
3. Give the closest microphone to the singer. The guitarist gets the clue from the singer when the verse ends.
4. You can then record the first take of the drums, the guitar, and the vocals.

5. Copy the guitar and the vocals and play them when the drummer records his takes

So, you have recorded the drums, the guitar, and the vocals but you don't feel good with the outcome. You can start overdubbing the guitar. Create a proper setup with the equipment for each instrument.

Tips for overdubbing

- *Be organized.* Come before the musicians do to prepare the equipment, like the microphones.
- *Plan ahead.* The musicians should know what they are supposed to do, but leave time allowance for some aspects of the recording. And, be sure that each musician knows his or her part before starting the record button.
- *Note the musicians' energy.* The artists should be comfortable when recording. Having them perform for numerous takes while you work on the set up will unnecessarily tire them.
- *White lies are acceptable.* White lies may become necessary to contain the artist, like when you say this is the last take and will not have the time for re-recording if they don't do it right.
- *Use a backup.* Make it a practice to have a backup, not only for overdubbing but for every work with the audio. Create backups of the session and save it to your spare hard drive when you are done or when your sessions end for the day.
- *Create multiple project files.* Another good practice to adapt is the use of multiple files. Do a "Save as" when you are going to make a big change, like consolidating compiled vocals. This method allows

you to go back to an earlier session if you missed something.
- *Have an organized session.* Get rid of the files you are not using, or make inactive channels that you think you will not need. But, before you do, make a "Save as"
- *Give importance to yourself.* Make sure you are comfortable with your workflow. If something is not right, breathe, be calm, and think of a solution.
- *Explore and experiment.* Do not hesitate to experiment. Try recording the kick drum through a bass guitar magnet and check the result. It would also do you good to be aware of your equipment and its limits.

6. Editing music

Editing music is a method of manipulating the sound to change the speed, length, volume, or to make additional versions of the original sounds. The amount of work you devote to music editing depends on the quality of the performances recorded. It follows that the better the performance, the lesser you have to edit music. This is why rehearsals are necessary.

The process of music editing

a. General editing

In general editing, you determine what works best from all the takes of performances recorded. For example, you recorded three vocals, you start by listening to all three recordings and decide which of the three vocals is the best. This choice shall be the take which you build on when you edit the rest of the parts.

Next is to find out if there are better recordings for sections of the song in other takes. For instance, after listening to the three tapes, you find out the 2nd take has a better performance of the bridge section.

Continue the process for each section until you have the best performance. When done, listen to the general edits you made to find out if the performance sounds believable and coherent. Check and match levels to assess that your decisions are not influenced by technical differences. Evaluate and note for sections which you believe need further editing work before going on to the next stage of the editing process.

When evaluating your work, write down your notes using a spreadsheet. Write each line of the song on the lyric column. You can use x and y to note that the line works (x) or does not work (y). Or, you can use your own codes to make notes about each song line.

b. Medium editing

You do medium editing when you find that there are remaining issues to resolve from the general editing. It is possible that upon reviewing the general editing, you discover that there are still certain phrases, words, or sections that need more attention.

Start this process by taking whole phrases. For example, you may listen to the feel and attitude when looking into the quality of the song, instead of the pitch. You may need to grab a word or two from other takes, but make sure that they match sonically. You can start solving the issue one at a time.

c. Fine editing

Before going to the fine editing stage, try to listen to the overall song with a fresh ear. Have your full attention on the whole song and not on the parts. Often, when we listen to a part over and over, we tend to notice the minute parts and forget the overall feeling of the song. The "feel" should be the most important part of the evaluation.

Once you are through listening to the whole song, you can start listening to the finer details. Pick out the issues, start with the issue that is most obvious and continue from there.

7. Music Mixing

The art of music mixing is considered the most difficult and critical part of the whole music production process. This is why the professional sound engineer gets the highest paying job in music production. If you are a novice sound engineer or music producer, it helps to listen to other mixes you happen to like and figure out what makes the mix good.

Take notes; write down the impression you get from the song. Is the feeling you get from listening to the song that of depression, jealousy, or love? Close your eyes and picture the music. Listen to an instrument and figure out where it is coming from. Does the instrument sound far or close? Is it low or loud? Is the sound distorted or clear? What are the effects used to support the emotion of the song?

Studying mixes has its merits. You can learn how to create templates out of studying mixes of songs. Then you can create your own style.

The basics of music mixing

Sound mixing is a process where you collate recorded tracks and blend them together. You can use various processes when mixing, such as EQ, Reverb, and Compression.

The purpose of mixing is to extract the best in your multitrack recording with the end-view of shaping your music to make its sense and meaning clear to listeners.

A multitrack recording is a recording with more than one track, also called as stems. The end output of multitrack recording is referred to as the mixdown, which is also your last step before mastering.

Before you start with the actual process, you have to prepare your work environment:

- Choose your equipment for mixing. Have a Digital Audio Workstation (DAW) to get you started. There are a lot of DAWs in the market to choose from, but choose the best that works for you. Once you have selected or purchased one, stick to it and get to know your DAW well. With a DAW, you can record live or virtual instruments and vocals, you can do audio looping, editing, mixing, and do audio effects.

- Set up the mixing session. If you are new to DAW, this software is equipped with templates to help you get started. There are templates for different instruments. If you don't find one that you want, you can create your own template. Making your own template is great in creating your own style.

- Label your tracks. Naming your tracks can prove handy when you need to go over your work after a couple of months. For example, if you are going to record a lead guitar, name it properly as 'lead guitar' before you start recording.
- Use color coding to identify track groups. Color coding helps you when doing processes on, for instance, bussing and identifying layers in your session. This tips will save you valuable hours in searching for the material

You are now ready to start with mixing. Here are the processes involved:

a. *Levels and panning.*

Organize your tracks. Group tracks that work together in the mix. Position each group that complements the song next to each. This saves you from too much movement in your mix window. Your mindset in this step is to consider the relative distance (the levels) and placement (the panning) of the instruments.

For example, if the lead vocals is the focus in your mix, make sure the placement of the other instruments is complementary to the vocals. If the placement if faulty, the instruments will get in the way or lose the attention to the vocals. It is advisable to start placement with the big instrument, like bass and drums.

b. Discard and edit.

After you have organized your tracks, remove what is unnecessary. This may include discarding the hiss or low frequency rumble, muting or removing performances that cloud the production or does not work, doing subtractive EQ, and editing areas that have no music.

This step in the process gives you the opportunity to enjoy the details of single performances. And, discarding and editing is also crucial as this gives you more space, flexibility, and room for your creativity.

When you are done with this step, adjust the levels to make up for the changes you made. Adjusting the levels is necessary since by removing the trash, this clears up the other tracks and may sound louder in the mix. Further, when you use the subtractive EQ, the tracks may turn out lower in sound and needs to be raised.

c. Compression

Audio compression when recording, it reduces the range of your dynamics. It does so by lowering the level of the loudest parts which brings the quiet parts closer to the loud in volume. The result is that the natural volume variations are not that obvious.

In the compression stage, you are actually controlling the dynamic range. The compressor unit sets the limit on the amount of frequency gets through. With the quieter sound boosted and the loud parts lowered, you achieve a consistent and balanced sound.

Take care not to be carried away with audio compression. Too much compression can be a danger to the mix. Using compression only to balance levels can make the sound lifeless. Use it with volume to get the best results.

d. Processing effects.

Effect is a device that treats the sound in a certain way and adds it back to an untreated or dry version of the audio.

In effects processing, you will often hear the terms wet and dry sounds. Wet sounds refer to processed sound which is done through a device. The dry sounds are untreated or unprocessed sounds and the source of the wet sounds. The wet sounds have different effects that the recorder can choose from. These effects come in three categories: frequency-based, dynamics-based, and time-based.

The frequency-based signal manipulates the frequency, such as equalizers and distortions. The dynamics-based effect changes the sounds dynamic levels. Examples are expanders, maximizers, and limiters. The time-based effect comprises a delay which include reverbs, flangers, echoes, choruses, and phasers.

e. Shaping the sound

Despite your effort to set the depth, tone, and balance, often there will still be issues that remain. This is where EQ can be of great help to you. The equalizer is, basically, a problem-solving tool. It enable you to cut or add the volume of specified frequencies. You can use the equalizer in many ways to resolve issues created during the recording session or right incompatibilities in instruments. You can also use it in creative ways to come up with original effects.

Before making use of equalizers, it helps to know the following concepts: one is that equalizers are used as inserts on channels, not as sends, and two is that you need to know the most common equalizers in a DAW.

There are five categories of equalizers that are commonly used:

1. Peak – is versatile. It is used to cut, or boost a frequency. It is usual to use it in the center of the frequency spectrum.
2. High shelf - This is used in the middle to high end. It is effective in brightening up a track. Use with caution because it can raise the overall noise of a track.
3. Low shelf – this is used between low to middle and low range of the spectrum. This equalizer minimizes some of the noise coming from low frequency sources.
4. High pass – refers to a drastic filter that is used to cut the very low noises which is below 60Hz.
5. Low pass – This is also a drastic filter used to reduce high frequencies noises. Take care in using this type to avoid overcutting the high presence of the sound.

Here are some things to remember about EQ:

- It is a procedure to solve problems. It helps if you know your goal and how you want the final result to sound.

- Bear in mind to make minor changes each time you add sounds to your mix. This is because changes in frequency and ranges of instruments affect the sound of them.
- You should be able to highlight the main frequencies you are working on. You should also be able to eliminate those frequencies that do not enhance the sonic features.
- Generally, it is safer to cut instead of to boost. The reason is because it is generally cleaner.

Rules to guide you in EQ:

1. The gain parameter of the EQ should be set at a reasonable level.
2. Do not boost or cut by more than 6dB, except when you think it is necessary. If your EQ settings are over this limit, check the reason for the excess in limit and find a solution.
3. If you find yourself in the situation where cutting or boosting frequencies at the same time

f. Grouping instruments

There are many ways of grouping in audio mixing. The most common methods used are mix grouping and audio grouping.

Mix grouping is the most popularly used by recorders. The concept of this grouping is to alter the level or mute state of all group members. Before you do mix grouping, however, be sure you have a balance of your audio and the sounds approximate what you have in mind. This reminder is important since a change in balance of one member, for instance, will also change the balance of the other members in the group.

Audio grouping is where you bus all members of the group in a single track. This way, you can process them together in their stereo mix form. A group bus is where you combine all tracks and sent or merged so you can do collective action on them. The idea of audio grouping is to:

- have groups of instruments to be processed at the same time
- make it easy to create mix stems for remixing
- create mix with simple variations

g. Printing the final mix

You are fortunate that the last step in the mixing process is less stressful than it was in the past. Pro Tools 48 track mix bounces back easily after loading the session file. You can then revisit the mix at any time with the expectation that is exactly as it was.

Take caution, however, because the biggest advantage of a computer-based audio mixing is also its biggest disadvantage. Since you find it easy to restore the audio mix, the mixing process can go on and on. This could result to a final mix that has lost its uniqueness and character. You need to stop at some point and let it go. Then move on to create new music.

When you have made up your mind to print the final mix, be sure to print the individual mix stems. Printing stems can come in handy if, for example, you have to send these to remixers who prefer to have groupings of instruments isolated for sample purposes. They are also helpful if the mastering engineer have problems with your mixes. It is easy for the mix stems to be lumped together in the mastering computer where instruments can be processed separately.

8. Mastering

Mastering is the last step in the long process of music production. It is a post-production process where the album or audio mix is prepared for distribution. It is, therefore, also considered as the initial stage in the manufacture process. The practice has been in the music industry since the early 1900s and had evolved with the changes brought by the advancing technology. It has gone through technical changes from the 33 1/3 and 45 rpm to audio cassettes, CDs, and the mp3s.

During the early practice of audio engineering, the purpose was to beat technical limitations and come up with a master that is close to the original mix. Through the mastering engineers Bob Ludwig, Bernie Grundman, and Doug Sax, the mastering was transformed into a creative process in the late 1970s.

Preparing the master mixes

The final mixes are delivered to master engineers in a format. Starting with the multitrack recording, the format used was the analog tape. Toward the 1980s, final mixes were in the format of reel to reel tape and recorded on digital tapes. With the development of computer technology in the 1990s, the hard drive or a hard disc was the medium used to send final mixes to the master engineers.

With whatever medium used, the format must be one that the mastering engineer can work on. It is the responsibility of the mastering engineer to manage the masters using the discerning ear to judge if the masters can be processed and what method to use.

For the medium used:

- Analog tape masters - should have a tone reel to align the tape machine electronics. When aligned, transferring masters can be done accurately.
- Digital tape masters – should be viewed for counting errors, as well as clocking issues and dropouts that cause masters to be degraded.
- Computer-based mixes – should be evaluated for sample rate, file format, and bit depth to check for the best quality format.

The transfer process

In recent years, the transfer process for mastering has been simplified when the final mixes were sent to mastering engineers as digital audio files. This method eliminated the need to convert analog to digital audio files.

Converting analog to digital was viewed by some mastering engineers as the weakest link in the mastering process. This has been the subject of debate for long. It is, therefore, not surprising to see mastering engineers convert the digital files to analog before submitting back to the mastering program and be processed.

With the vinyl tape as the medium for mastering audio, the work process was simple. The final mixes were organized into two reels (side A and B). Spacing or editing was done using the razor blade to splice the tape. This is then submitted to the mastering console to be processed and leveled.

Transfer process is simpler for vinyl tapes. The mastering engineers organize the final mixes to two reels, side A and B. The spacing and editing are done by a razor blade and splicing tape as mentioned above. When done, the final masters are transferred in real time to the lacquer, one side at a time.

In case of downloadable releases and CDs, processing starts with the analog tapes using equalizers and compressors before converting them to digital. The decision on how to process the transfer would depend on the type of method sound best for the engineer. Whatever the method used, the decisions should be based on how best to preserve the original quality of the final mixes.

<u>Setting the order of the song</u>

It is common for mastering engineers to import songs as they appear on the CD. There is a reason why mastering engineers would divert from this practice. One is due to the medium used to transfer them, and the other could be because of compatibility between analog and selected tracks. But, once the transfer is done to the mastering program, changing the song order will not affect any level of editing or processing.

Weighing the order of the song is an important decision. The mastering engineer must focus on the ordered flow of the songs on a CD. A strong song usually starts the order on a CD; it does not have to be the single that is played for radio and promotion. The listeners may not go through the CD if the best songs are played early. But a coherent order of the songs will draw fans toward enjoying all the songs on the CD.

Editing

After transferring the masters, edit the files for a clean start and end of each song. For a smooth transition from silence, it is usual to have a short breath of space at the start of a song then a fade-out. Editing the end of a song involves removing extra noises, then again, have a fade-out for a natural conclusion.

Preparing the final mixes for mastering, it is best to supply the mixes with extra room at the beginning and end of the song. This technique gives the mastering engineer something to work with. Often, mastering engineers receive mixes with clipped heads and tails. This means extra work for mastering engineers who will have to find ways to make the beginning and ending of the song sound natural.

Setting space between songs

The space between songs defines the order of the record from start to. In defining the space, the artist and producer collaborate to determine that the next song's entry sounds natural. A hard hitting track may need a longer space if the next song feels lighter. Dance records usually line up the following song to begin with a virtual downbeat making it sound like the previous song's tempo continues through the space in between.

Processing

You can do processing in audio mastering when it is necessary. When processing, the motto for the mastering engineer is to "do no harm." Processing is done through equalizers and compressors, though these forms can also serve other purposes.

If used lightly, compressors add power and level to a mix. Compressors can also control or limit peak levels to increase song's overall gain. As a multi-band compressor, it helps to strengthen a frequency area that is flawed in the mix.

The equalizers also serve many uses in mastering audio. It can be used in a subtle way to shape a frequency area in the mix to enhance depth and clarity. EQ can filter out low frequencies that sound muddy or lack punch. You can also use the notch filter to remove annoying frequencies in the mix.

Levels

In this step of the mastering process, make sure all levels are even from one song to another. Uneven balances can result from frequency density, frequency content, and compression amount. Let your ear be the judge to get the balance. Further, the use of fade in and fade out can alter the recognized level of the subsequent song. The distinction between the actual and perceived level can result to faulty decisions if you only look at meters for your reference.

The sonic maximizer is handy as a limiter form. It controls fleeting peak signals. It can also let signals that are below the ceiling to increase its levels. The purpose is similar for each plug in, that is, to have it as loudly as possible without altering or destroying the mix. The sonic maximize is the most overused (read: abused) tool in mastering audio today to get the perceived level.

ID tags and PQ coding

This process enables CD text, data copy protection, and UPC/EAN coding to enter the instructive data for the downloadable file or a CD. You can also identify digital audio files downloaded by its song name, songwriter, artist, musical style, date recorded, and other information through ID tagging. And, it has the advantage of letting the recordings' owner to track radio play and sales through ISRC and UPC/EAN coding.

Dithering

Dithering is great in preserving higher resolution masters quality. The dithering process is where you add random low-level noise to the sound when you go from 24 bit, and lower the bit depth to 16 bit needed during CD mastering. This aids in preserving depth sense in a mix found in higher masters bit depth. Dithering is considered the last step in mastering before finalizing and printing out the production master.

Final production master creation

The last stop in the mixing process is the final production master burning, which can either be a Disc Description Protocol (DDP) file or a PreMaster CD (PMCD). PMCD format is needed in manufacturing plants that are used in glass master creation. This requires the used of a CD media and a high quality disc burner to ensure that error counts are kept at a minimum.

Disc Description Protocol or DDP format is a type of data file containing all the pertinent data needed to create a glass master. A saved DDP file in your HDD can be directly uploaded to the website of the manufacturing plant. The DDP is widely accepted as more convenient and reliable as compared to PMCD.

The term glass master is so-called because the data is copied on a circular block of glass coated with a special chemical. It is also known as a "stamper." The process with glass master creation is what is also known as the CD+G, a standard disc Red Book. CD's burned through a computer have increased error counts.

Chapter 5. Inventions and Insights That Changed Music

Music is inherent in us, as seen in man's early history. It is one of man's first cultural expressions appearing before the age of agriculture and writing. As such, our early ancestors found means to produce music using the technology of their times, as evidenced by rudimentary forms of flute during the Paleolithic era of 40 thousand years ago.

Music has accompanied man throughout history. With man's innate creativity, the idea of music and technology became the means for our early ancestors to create new sound possibilities. We see these in historical records where music was produced in different formats and social functions, from religious rituals to breaking a worker's silence.

Since man changes with the conditions in the environment, the change also brought about changes in technology, how music is produced, the way music is recorded, how music is delivered to people, and how people listen to music. But, people continue to look for different ways to produce sound and experiment with various styles to express music which led to more advances in technology.

Expressing music through technology involves innovation and creativity. If you trace the history of music production and the advances in technology to create sound, you see a pattern from the early instruments sourced from perishable materials, to flutes using bones as material, lyres, and harps.

Today, the sound technology evolved into mechanical, electronic, and software devices used in producing the evolving sound. Music production, itself, evolved Into State-Of-The Art Devices.

Music Production VS Music Technology

Many tend to view the two terms, music production and music technology, as referring to the same concept. Both are necessary to the process of producing music, but each has a unique role.

A music producer tends to the logistical side of music production. This means organizing the studio to ensure that music is recorded; decide which songs appear on the record; coaching and giving directions to artists for desired sounds and appropriate techniques.

Music technology or audio engineering, as it is also called, is into the technical aspect of recording. Audio engineers are trained as specialists in the use of recording tools used in the studio. They are also adept in working with artists and musicians to get the best sound out of the technology.

The job of music production and technology are different, but they can be done by the same person. This is true, especially where the studio is small. With recording technology becoming democratized, both roles are accessible to more individuals. Assuming both roles give individuals creative control and influence on a record.

The Analogic Sound

The wax cylinder, shellac, and the radio
At the later part of the 19th century, people were already listening to an early form of audio recording, the most popular of which was the phonograph. The instrument was an

invention of Thomas Edison and introduced in 1877. The design consists of an acoustic cone, at the tip of which is a needle that scratched a wax cylinder as it moves around. Through a mechanical process, the needle vibrates as it moves on the grooves of the cylinder which case

During the same period, other technologies appeared, such as the gramophone shellac record which was invented in 1888 by Emile Berliner. The gramophone was placed by a disc. The quality of sound reproduction of these early models of records was limited and was, therefore used for recording monologues and speeches. Further, the task of recording from this instrument was sensitive, requiring the performance to be close to the cone that picks up the sound.

Another limitation with these instruments was that the acoustic cone was that it could only pick up the loudest sound. For example, the musical instruments that have less volume were placed near the cone. The louder the instruments' volume, the further they are from the cone. A recording trick done was to use a moving platform while playing. One other limitation of wax recording was that the product was fixed. A faulty performance cannot be fixed once performed.

At the onset of the next century, new inventions based on electric power appeared, changing how people access music. Radio became popular due to the development of the microphone and the electromagnetic waves. With the radio, anyone can listen to music and the news through a receiver. During this time, sound was based on real time performance done inside the studio. The quality of the music produced was far superior to that of the wax and shellac technology.

The Vinyl Records and the Magnetic Tape

The sound recording on magnetic came after World War II and was attributed as a German invention. The sound produced by this equipment was such that music produced was indistinguishable as live or recorded performances. After the war, the first magnetic tape was introduced in 1948. Broadcasting radios was quick to pick this new music technology and expanded the broadcasting possibilities. Hence, the recording studio was born.

In the same year the magnetic tape recording came out, vinyl recording appeared in the market. The first vinyl record was in 7" discs played at 78 rpm. This provides music playback for less than 4 minutes each side, and became the single compact format with one piece for each side. A setback of this format is that the vinyl grooves made volume limitations on bass frequencies; they result to needle jumps if played too loud. On the other hand, this limitation became the foundation for the pop and rock music.   The appearance of the vinyl record and the people's preference for this records gave birth to another phenomena – the rise of record companies.

The Studios and Technology
The recording studios were the means which gave rise to the new music industry. Studio spaces were acoustically treated, complex, and the process of producing music was costly. The experts in the industry would position microphones in front of the musicians. Several equipment were needed for the recording process, such as pre-amplifiers, equalizers, soundboards, compressors, and recording machines.

For four decades, the studio space was the only place where music was produced professionally, and at a high cost. Further, each studio had secrets in producing music, used unique equipment and methods, and stamped the records with their own personality.

The producers were creative in overcoming technical difficulties and limitations encountered which appeared in their projects. This ingenuity led to new techniques, expanded the horizons of music recording, and prompted other producers to come up with better solutions. The producers were creative in overcoming technical difficulties and limitations encountered which appeared in their projects. This ingenuity led to new techniques, expanded the horizons of music recording, and prompted other producers to come up with better solutions.

Les Paul modified the magnetic tape recorder which appeared in 1957. This invention created the first multiple-layer recorder where new instruments can be added on to the same roll. Since it was a single recording track, care was taken not to commit errors since it would mean restarting the whole process. The multitrack recorder was an improvement of the magnetic recorder. With this machine, they can record or delete independent tracks without affecting the others. An example of this king of multitrack is the songs of The Beatles. At the start of their career, they used four tracks of the magnetic tape. If an instrument is to be added, they would unite two or three tracks into one to free the space without changing other tracks. In the decades which followed, tapes grew to using eight up to twenty-four tracks.

The soundboard is another necessary equipment in the studio. It organized the audio tracks during recording sessions. Just like the recording machines, the soundboards evolved and kept pace with the growing number of tracks. Soundboard models were designed with hundreds of channels, with each channel having a dozen of sliders and control knobs. The equipment is housed in a cabinet which may be more than 3 meters long. For one not trained in this equipment, it could be intimidating. A magnetic tape track expert, however, can easily manipulate the sound in each channel before and after receiving the sound. This method allowed adjustments in volume and equalization, compression, and reverberation.

The adjustments made are part of mixing. In the mixing process, the adjustments are made in the channels. The instruments which are recorded separately sound cohesive when played at the same time. Further, the mixing of sound is for the stereo with left and right channels – a common format for vinyl records, CDs, and music digital files. There are several studios existing at the time, but the main difference for each is the equipment they use. A studio with many equalizers or compressors can have more mixing possibilities, though the cost is higher. And, because a studio is expensive, the use of professional music production is available only to those who controlled the market and those who can do greater musical projects.

The Commercial Sound

Recording companies were closed system in the music industry since the beginning. The composers were hired to compose new musical pieces and were recorded at the recording company's studio. The composer hired was usually popular, made so through the radio exposure. And because the composer is popular, this fact boosted sales and garnered huge profits for the recording company.

It was Frank Sinatra who was successful in being the first artist to have some measure of control over his career. With his status, he was able to enforce his will during recording sessions. Over the following years, other singer-composer and rock bands showed up.

On the business side, the process of commercial music production was expensive and risky. In addition to the recording process, other factors were involved, like the cost of record manufacture, marketing, distribution. Further, there was the possible loss of unsuccessful projects which the recording company absorbs.

On the flip side, the success of some artists earned capital that can be invested in other projects, leading to the development of new talents. Many rock bands of the 1970s were financed by the recording company or a producer, like the *Queen* or *Yes*.

Independent artists existed along with popular bands, but their influence was small. For independent artist to make a mark in the industry, they need to belong to a closed circuit of contract, marketing, distribution and massive sales. It was not until the advance of technology that independent artists existed outside the closed circuit scheme. An example of these artists were the Punk bands with their production of music done on cassette tape recorders which needed low studio resources.

At the start of music production, the materials of performers were released on compact singles which contained two songs, one song on each side. An example of this was Elvis Presley's singles'. The 12-inch record was done later, used initially for anthologies or niches, like the classical music. In the 1960s, bigger format was used by artists, like The *Beatles* and the *Beach Boys*. This bigger format was popular for the "concept albums" which contains a cohesive set of songs. This was followed by the rock and pop music, making the album as their main product.

With increasing sales, record companies expanded their reach and by the 1990s, the most saleable product were distributed and commercialized globally, setting up branches of record companies. The effect was an intensified new force – the recorded music. New sonorities began to influence musical characteristics, generating a new musical language.

The Digital Sound

At the close of the 1970s, sales of the vinyl records dropped and became a great concern of record companies. What saved the record companies was another technological innovation – the digital sound. Until 1982, reproducing and storing sounds were done in analogical way; that is, by physical printing of audio through mechanical and electromagnetic means. In the same year, the compact disc (CD) was introduced which used digitally represented data. In the 1980s and the 1990s, the digital format increased industry profits which due to low reproduction costs and increasing preference for pop music. With the CD, a listener is willing to pay more for this new media and can reacquire favorite albums in the digital disc version.

Before the 1980s and before the CD was released, sound recording was, in essence, analogic, that is, the use of magnetic tape, transistors, and valves. At the end of the 1970s, digital equipment got more space in studios, such as the board, processors, and recording equipment were gradually converted into the new technology.

How the analogic studio produces sound starts with the microphone picking up sound. The sound is then converted into electric waves, which pass through wires and equipment. The electric waves are then changed and manipulated by the soundboard, processors, and lastly, recorded on magnetic tape.

Sound production in a digital studio is different. The sound is represented by numbers describing the sound wave behavior. The audio processors are formulated by algorithms, operating mathematically to change the sound.

Understanding The Difference Between Analog And Digital Sound Recording

You will understand analog and digital recording by comparing the two. The analog recording makes use of methods that copies the original sound waves. Examples of medium for this type of recording are the vinyl records and the cassette tapes. The digital recording takes samples of the original waves at a stated rate. Examples of digital mediums are MP3 and CDs.

The potential reliability of the analog recording relies on the equipment's sensitivity and the type of medium used for recording and playback. On the other hand, the reliability of digital audio relies on the rate at which the recording machine sampled the original sound wave over a specified time.

Despite the latest techniques and technologies, digital audio cannot come up with exact replications of the original sound wave. Digital audio companies attempt to hide this limitation with words like "Lossless" and "Uncompressed." The words are misleading since all digital audio have a few loss of original signals and compression. These limitations, however, are undetected even by the trained ear and fail to detect the difference between the analog audio and high-quality digital signals.

Computers In Sound Recording

As time went on and with the advance in technology, studios became homogenized and differentiation through equipment can no longer apply. Computers increasingly played an active role in the sound recording process.

In 1982, the IBM PC-XT device can perform 20 mathematical operations per second. A modern personal processor followed suit after thirty years, with a capacity to operate a thousand times faster. The speed of processors is the key to use complex algorithms, which brings out digital effects that are close to analogic recording. The computer has a bigger advantage in that its digital recreation can be used in an indefinite number of times and simultaneously. Another advantage of the computer is its capacity to simulate hissings and noises and turn off at any time, a feature that the original equipment cannot do.

Support technologies came to be used in studios. One is the soundboard, which is a central piece of analogic configuration. It is a highly complex and expensive equipment where all the channels pass. The soundboard is manipulated by controls and buttons, which then manages electrically the sound that come from or is directed to the magnetic tape.

The computer is the main tool in a digital studio, the soundboard the controller. with its sliders and knobs which merely sends digital instructions to the computer. The soundboard can be smaller or may even be viewed as obsolete. This can then be replaced by a mouse and keyboard shortcuts.

With the advance of technology, what used to be inaccessible is fast becoming affordable to non-professional musicians and artists. The soundboards and the magnetic tapes can now be replaced by a personal computer, microphones price are low, and it is now possible to record a whole piece of music by simply using a notebook.

What adds to the computer's popularity is its easy manipulation of digital audio. Then, with the magnetic tape, putting two recording requires to look for the slices of tape one wants to use, cut and glue them together. With the computer program now, the digital audio simply clicks and drags the it and paste on the desired section without altering the original material. With the computer, synchronizations and inversions are done faster than the old techniques.

With each advance in technology, the computer programs designed to make, record, change, and mix have evolved efficiently, replacing the previous physical equipment. Today, sound production is made with the computer as the main tool.

The Virtual Sound

The internet became popular in the 1990s, which led to the development of various technologies. In addition to the communication interface, the modems, servers, and networks enhanced the methods for transmitting data through the internet. GIF and JPG compressed image file formats grew in popularity and it was not long after the audio transfer solutions appeared.

It was the introduction of the MP3 which greatly changed audio file size, having the capacity to reduce it to 8% of its original size. Reduction of size, however, resulted to a much lower quality of sound. In 1995 when this format was popular, the loss of quality was not as important for the listeners than the opportunity to exchange music online.

Chapter 6. The Transformation of Music

We are at an era where we don't have to own a record or a disc to enjoy music. We have but to stream music and we can listen to our choice of song. It may be easy for us to choose the song we want and to listen to it, but it has not always been like this. The road that led music to where it is today is laden with history.

The musical formats have been with us since the 1870s. Each evolution has its own reason the making. Some of these musical formats may have been efficient while some were not. But, it is these dissatisfactions which became the stepping stones to a much improved format.

Most people today go for the digital format – download or streaming – and has done away with records. The digital format is so prevalent that many musicians gave up the physical formats. We cannot, however, ignore the fact that every format which appeared played an important role in the development of music formats today.

The Record (1948)

The earliest recording of sound known was in April 9, 1860 done on a phonoautograph. This machine was invented by Édouard-Léon Scott de Martinville, a French typesetter.

It was designed to record sounds visually and not for playback. The purpose for recording sound was to record speech that can be deciphered later. In the same year, Scott recorded his voice and is believed to be the first recorded human voice in history. There was no playback then. It was in 2008 when scientists reproduced his recorded voice.

Scott's device was designed with a horn shaped like a barrel which was attached to a stylus. The stylus etched the sound waves on paper sheets blackened by an oil lamp's smoke.

In 1948, records with varying speeds came out. This was the first music format. The early version of this format was the 78 RPM made of shellac, which material made it noisy. Columbia records later created the 33 RPM Long Play format or LP. This was followed by RCA's 45 RPM Extended Play format, also called EP. Columbia and RCA, however, looked for alternative to the fragile shellac material and invented the Vinyl records.

The Compact Cassette Tape (1963)

Philips Company developed the compact cassette tape in 1962 and was released in August 30, 1963 during the Berlin Radio Show in . It was small in size and affordable. The use of the tape gave rise to the invention of the portable player, considered to be a major development in physical format's history. The tape's playing time was 45 minutes each side, much longer than the previous formats.

The negative side of this invention was the emergence of piracy, an issue which the music industry faces until now. The tapes, however, had its positive side as this became the path to the development of mix tapes which evolved to today's playlists.

8 Track Tape (1964)

This tape was the result of the collaboration between RCA records and Lear Jet Company. The advantage of the 8 track tape over the compact cassette was its storage. The 8 track tape has the capacity to store eight soundtracks and four audio programs. This format came out after the war. The automobile industry then was booming, and Ford offered the 8 track tape in their car as an option.

Car owners enjoyed listening to music while driving. This format enjoyed a short-lived popularity, from 1968 to 1975. The slump was caused by problems with the format. The 8 track tape was found to be unreliable, with loss of sound quality over time, and they were expensive. The casing was durable, but the internal parts were made out of cheap materials which broke easily.

The Floppy Disc (1972)

When you hear of the concept of floppy disc, what comes to mind is data storage for desktop computers. During the 1980s and the 1990s though, artists used the floppy disc to release their albums.

This 8 inch floppy disc was released by IBM in 1972, followed by a 5-1/4 inch version in 1976, and a 3-1/2 inch format in 1982. This music format never really hit the mainstream. There were few attempts to give floppy discs a multimedia angle, but did not catch on. Except for one notable release, Brian Eno's album, the Generative Music I (1996) released through Opal Music.

The floppy disc may not be a success as a music format, but it is still important in foreshadowing the digital future of music.

The Compact Disc (1982)

Philips had been exploring the idea of a compact disc since 1974. During the same time, Sony was also on the same idea, working on a CD to replace the tape and disc. Using multiple optical mediums, Sony and Philips finalized the CD and formulated the Red Book standards for audio CD. The Red Book is a series of books containing the technical specs for CD formats.

The CD was first released in 1982 and offered to the greater public in 1983. With the CD, the CD player was invented, the first of which was the Sony CDP 101. Through the years after its introduction, CD sales exploded.

A contributory factor for the CD format's popularity is the timely release of Dire Strait's album, *Brothers in Arms*. The album was recorded in the latest digital technology, the outcome of which decided Philips to sponsor a tour. The CD was released in May 1985 and became popular among fans and audio lovers. Add to CD's increasing sales is the following features: high-quality audio, portable, compact, inexpensive, and writable.

The MP3 (1992)

MP3 is short for MPEG-1 Audio Layer III. This technology was approved for use in 1991 and published in 1993. The idea behind MP3 was the perceptual limits of human hearing, also known as auditory masking. Auditory masking is the effect a listener gets where a faint sound is not heard due to the presence of a louder sound. Another hearing limitation is that a song has audio elements that are not perceptible to the listening experience.

The use of psychoacoustic algorithm for audio was first used by Manfred R. Schroeder and Bishnu S. Atal in 1978. This algorithm made use of the masking characteristics of the human ear. But, it was in 1988 with the formation of the ISO MPEG Audio Group that an audio coding global standard was reached.

Another significant name in MP3 history is Karlheinz Brandenburg. He started his work on digital music compression in 1980, centering on the way people perceive music. Brandenburg finished his doctoral work in 1989. He continued his work on digital music compression and used Susanne Vega's song, the "Tom's Diner" to develop MP3. He used the song to test and refine his scheme, making sure the procedure did not affect Vega's voice adversely.

The song "Tom's Diner" was selected as the test music because of its almost monophonic characteristic and broad spectral content. These features make it easy to detect imperfections in the compression format when played back. This is how Susanne Vega came to be called "The mother of MP3."

The advantages and disadvantages of MP3 technology
The internet has made the use of MP3 popular. And, there are software available which allow MP3 users to choose the bit rate when converting audio files into MP3 file format. The bit rate one chooses affects the quality of the sound. Bit rates come within the range of 96 to 320 kilobits per second (Kbps). The sound quality that you hear which is like what you hear from a radio uses the 128 kbps. If you prefer to hear sounds that are close to the quality of a CD music, a bit rate of 160 kbps is recommended.

There are, however, others who say that MP3 sound does not afford you the best means to experience music. They argue that despite the high bit rate setting, MP3 audio files are inferior to CDs and vinyl records. By knowing the advantages and disadvantages, you would know if the MP3 file is for you.

The benefits

- Low audio file size which allows you to rip more music files on a disc.

- A flexible compression ratio which gives you the freedom to choose the compression rate to your desired size. Less compression rate offers better quality but a bigger file size.

- Less expensive distribution of music.

- Easy file sharing on the internet or a physical medium, like the CD or USB.

- Eliminates the need for a studio recording, giving opportunities for artists and musicians (new and veterans) to promote their music.

- Downloads and uploads are significantly faster, unlike earlier technologies where it take hours to download music.

- MP3s can be played with many audio players, such as iPods, CD players, Windows media player, Winamp, or QuickTime.

- An ID3 tag which stores the name of the artist, song title, genre, and the year. It also allows you to come up with your own playlists.

- The digital format of MP3 allows you to create several copies of the same file without affecting the quality of the sound. This method is referred to as serial duplication.

The drawbacks

- The major disadvantage is its low audio quality. The lossy algorithm used in audio compression removes the "lesser" audible content, affecting the quality of music recorded.

- Ease of use and accessibility of this music technology led to music piracy, which through the years, has increased to a great extent.

- Data is open to losses because of virus attack or malware. For instance, users of Morpheus – a file-sharing service – can easily be accessed by hackers.

Streaming (2002)

The exponential growth of the internet gave entrepreneurs and developers the opportunity to make music easily accessible to the public. With streaming, online users can get to listen to music without breaking the law or the need to store large amount of data. Streaming music then grew to become an industry giant. On the other hand, the emergence of streaming led to the decline of revenue for MP3 and CDs.

Streaming platforms were developed for the purpose of making digital music a business model that can be sustained. Software applications developed for desktop became easily available. Streaming soared, especially with the launching of iPhone in 2007, and the launching of software applications like Spotify, the first on-demand service online.

Streaming opened another chapter for format – the dematerialized music format.

Chapter 7. How Modern Technology Has Changed Music Production Forever

What used to be an artistic market, the music industry went through constant restructuring of the recording practices ever since sound reproduction was invented in the late 19th century. During the 1900s, record and broadcast companies chose the artists they would manage, finance, and promote.

With the coming of the digital technology, music no longer need to depend on record companies and gave rise to independent production. By the end of 1990s, the internet and its increasing use for music sharing led to the decrease of the traditional business model of music production.

Presented with the present environment, the challenge for music producers was to reinvent music production using the technology of today. Knowing what changes occurred and how these changes interact with the present and evolve into something new may provide insights that will help aspiring musicians, artists, and producers face these challenges.

Effect Of Sound Reproduction

The origin of sound recording can be traced back to 1876 when Alexander Graham Bell and Thomas Watson came up with a process that captured sound. Two years after, the wax cylinder, which stored captured sounds, was invented. In 1877, an apparatus for recording sound and reproduction was described by Charles Cros, a French inventor and poet, and was introduced a year later by Thomas Alva Edison. This device became known as the phonograph.

With the invention of these devices, captured sound became fixed and immortalized through sound reproduction techniques – the recording of sound. Like in photography where people adapt their gestures and looks after seeing themselves, in music, singers and musicians can listen to their performance objectively and adapt their interpretation. The performers started to experiment with new modes of expression with the use of the microphone. The microphone then became an instrument in its own right.

From the standpoint of the listeners, recorded music and live performance brings about different listening experiences. Recorded music can be listened to in private, even in the midst of distractions. The listener can change its volume or switch music off anytime.

Capturing sound into recorded music, therefore, transformed music from the time dimension into the space dimension. This transformation has the effect of inspiring composers to compose music that is not too subtle nor too complicated for single listening.

With the geographically widespread distribution of recorded music, this has led to transformation in the way music was composed and performed. Exposure to foreign musical practices led to the emergence of musical movements, one of which is jazz. Studio practices likewise changed the musician's language and methods. According to Hennion (1981), it is at the arrangement through orchestration, recording, and mixing phases that a tune becomes meaningful. To cite an example, jazz was composed by recordings. Jazz performers learn to play their music by listening to and copying recorded music. From here, performers develop their own instrumental technique.

To sum up the effect of sound recordings, recorded music influenced made dramatic impact on musicians and performers. On the flip side, recordings gave listeners new ways to experience music. With more people listening to recorded music today, the quality of the sound recorded could make or break music produced.

Aesthetic Approaches To Music Production

In the early stages of sound recording, the technical limitations encountered by sound engineers drove them to come up with creative methods to capture sound through placement of microphones close to the source. It was during the First World War that electrical recording techniques were introduced. This technique allowed boosting of microphone signals and aided by playback on loudspeakers.

Improved recording quality increased sales of recorded music, which, in turn, motivated the industry to produce more of the higher-quality recordings. With the electrical recording technique, sound engineers can place microphones further from the sources and capture the natural room reverberation. This method created what is referred to as "a metaphor of presence" or the illusion of listening to a live performance rather than in the living room. It was Leopole Stokowski who pioneered in the use of electrical recordings.

In 1931, Columbia Records introduced the Long Playing discs which allowed longer pieces to be recorded. Further, improvements in the microphone technology resulted to the invention of stereophony in the 1940s, motivating record engineers to explore new techniques. The goal of the record engineers was to create a stereo image instead of having the focus on fidelity of sound. Advances in technology offered sound engineers the use of multiple microphones and mix them during recording. This method was a challenge for sound engineers to match their techniques with musical aesthetics.

The Challenge Of Editing Takes And Mixing Tracks

The magnetic tape recording was introduced towards the end of World War II, and transformed recording studios into something more like musical instruments. The appearance of the tape led to three techniques for musical production:

- Editing music by cut and paste
- changing short musical passages by overwriting them over previous track recordings. This was referred to as *punch in* technique.
- Multitrack recording which enabled sound engineers to mix tracks sourced from multiple microphones during postproduction

These improvements in techniques increased studio practices and generated the need for editing and mixing. These in turn expanded the role of music producers to include control and supervision of the reconstruction of music during postproduction.

The following are examples of artists who pioneered the use of creative postproduction techniques: Glenn Gould who believed that postproduction or posttaping overcomes the limitations of the performer in the personal interpretation of music; Miles Davis who made his music by recording extended improvisations and then submitting his composition to his producer, Teo Macero, for editing and reassembling according to Davis' wishes; and, The Beatles who collaborated with their

producer, George Martin. By minimizing sound editing, the final product appears to be closer to a live performance. On the other hand, editing to construct a musical piece creates a virtual performance. Editing and mixing led to three kinds of recordings (Edidin, 1999):
1) Recording performance which is the capturing the fluidity of the performance, that is, not being fixed in time;
2) Composite recordings of compositions referring to the use of editing and mixing
3) Recording artifacts where an art work could not have been performed. For instance, a guitar instrument overdubbing three synchronized guitar parts.

The technologies introduced in the 1980s broadened the possibilities of the third kind of recording – the recording artifacts – which opened unlimited transformation capabilities with the use of the Music Instrument Digital Interface protocol (MIDI), the Digital Audio Workstations (DAW), and the digital correction tools and multi audio effects with the capacity to change time, pitch, reverberation, and be rid of unwanted noise.

The Changing Business World Of The Music Industry

The record companies control of artists
Not only did sound recording changed the way people listen to music, but benefitted the recording industry with increased revenue due to the production of the disc. The mass production of the discs kept revenue increasing, mostly attributed to the 'teenager' market. Another factor contributing to the success of the recording industry at this time was the increase in the number of labels and record companies. Diversity and innovation usually emerges in the

midst of a competitive market. Such environment points to a satisfactory supply to a broad range of music lovers.

At this point, the recording companies were able to have more control over music production and recordings. Also at this time, technology gained prominence in importance than musicality. The effect was to have the rock musicians getting more involved in the audio mixing process, but with the lessening of control by the sound mixer in the recording process. This gave rise to the problem of shared responsibilities and roles in the recording process.

Another effect was the drop in numbers of record companies, and what remained were the major ones. In the 1970s, the recording industry experienced a decline in sales and in the percentages of new artists. This down slope of the recording industry was caused by the introduction of the audio cassette in the early 1970s. This new device encouraged music listening in private and also promoted piracy.

Along this time, record companies gained more control over artists, which affected the diversity and quality of music production. One transformation which occurred was musicians working from home without the need of collaboration from major labels. This was made possible by the 4- and 8-track tape devices which were cheap and portable. But, there were also artists who went back to record labels to take advantage of their marketing strategies and the expertise of their engineers and producers.

Delocalization of recording studios
The 1980s found the introduction of Compact Disc (CD) which caused sales of recordings to rise once more. Though initially a positive event for the recording industry, the CD, however,

caused major upheavals in terms of changes in studio practices and delocalization of recording studios.

The affordable digital sound equipment and the fear of losing control over their artistic creations moved the musicians to create music in their homes – the so-called bedroom studios. The effect was doing away with specialized studio professions, such as editor, recording engineer, and other specialized professions which correspond to the stages of music production. This gave way for the multi-skilled professionals who handled the whole music production process.

There was another technology introduced which was the force behind the change in the 1980s – the MIDI and its massive use by artists and musicians. This technology enabled musicians to compose with synthetic sounds rather than recording performers. Most often the synthetic sounds are factory presets. With the appearance of digital technologies in this decade, the number of independent productions soared.

The digital technologies, however, have their limitations. Music recording output of digital technologies cannot compare with the sound quality which results from professional recording. Nor is it comparable to the artistic abilities of a real musician playing with the room's acoustics.

It was in the 1990s when the internet was developed and opened new potentialities for organizing work. At this point, recordings began to be produced in network studios, where home studios that are geographically distant were connected and functioned as nodes in a network. With the network, engineers and artists could send individual tracks and pre-mixes to associates and collaborators at any stage of the production process. This means, people involved in the production process, though located in different geographical areas, can work together without the need of a face-to-face meeting.

Downturn of the traditional business model of recording companies

When the lossy compressed audio format was invented, this encouraged peer-to-peer exchange of musical digital files through MP3. Though piracy already existed with the invention of the cassette, exchange of audio files with the digital technology was in a larger scale. The massive scale of copying and transferring music reduced the recording companies revenue significantly. The International Federation of the Phonographic Industry (IFPI) reports that from 2004 and 2011, sales from recordings fell by 31%.

What contributed to the loss of sales of recording companies were the specialized search engines, unlicensed download sites, forums, cyberlockers, newsgroups, and blogs, including the peer-to-peer exchange that requires no payment. Add to this the willingness of artists of streaming to promote their music via social networks.

To sum it up, the internet changed the way music lovers access music. With this kind of environment, the quality of the sound is not the selling point. One can copy audio files, but with the lossy compression, some parts of the video frames and sound waves are irretrievably lost when decompressed. Since quality is no longer important to listeners, artists and record companies lost the interest to invest in music production. But, there are those who are concerned with the loss of sound quality. In an attempt to restore sound quality, sound engineers came up with high-resolution audio digital formats.

The commercialized versions of the high-resolution audio format are the DVD-audio, SACD, and the Blu-ray.

The new business model had the following effects:
- Major recording companies no longer invested in the development of a new artist's career.
- Local artists signed to labels reduced dramatically
- Record labels stopped listening to music demos and turned to acts that were already established in the market
- Contracts with labels were only for the distribution of albums produced entirely by musicians
- Downturn in record labels led to more creativity and artistic freedom

Chapter 8. The Professional Art of Critical Listening

Being critical of another's work is one way of learning one's trade or profession. For a music practitioner, to appreciate a musician's creation and critical about the work is necessary if one is to learn. To be critical in listening to music is a must for personal development in the field of music, and in developing a personal style.

Being critical does not mean disapproval or negative criticism, but a professional and academic approach. One can view critical analysis as a means to benchmark the audio or music you are listening to, and use this to construct your music in the future. Critical analysis should also include how your musical creation fits the genre and how it is representative of the times.

It is not easy to come up with a proper opinion of recorded music. The key word here is "proper" and is the term that makes forming an opinion difficult. But, these opinions make you who you are and allow you to engage in discussions on your subject matter. Though forming a proper opinion is difficult, this ability can be learned.

Balancing Objectivity and subjectivity

One might ask: What is a proper opinion?
It is natural that emotions come in when forming an opinion. However, emotions should not dominate you, but guide you in making an opinion. Being objective is a desirable trait, whatever your profession or position is. Objectivity is seeing and understanding the other person's point of view.

Learning how to be objective, balanced with subjectivity, can help you greatly in your career. For instance, producers often speak of a vibe in music to boost its attraction. The creation of a vibe could be based on an emotional response of the producer. The producer may go with this emotion and let it guide the session. But, it is *objectivity* which prevails, serving as the reality check during the production process, working on it within the context of current trends and marketability.

A way to test a balanced opinion is to put yourself as one of the buying public. Check yourself if the music moves you to dance or to rock your head. These may seem irrational responses to you, but they serve as the triggers that make you a musician, a producer, or a music lover. These irrational responses, when you think about it, can give you insights that would help you become a producer.

Emotions will always be with you, but to be able to control your emotions may prove to be of great value for you as a producer or a musician. You may hear people telling you to separate emotions from your work and be wholly objective in opinions and decisions. But, music is different, especially in music production.

Music is an art form, but to make and produce music is a product, therefore, saleable. Music production, therefore, combines the art form with the market. It is something that you create with love and attention, later to be sold in the market for your benefit.

Forming an opinion is crucial to an aspiring music producer or musician. It is your proper opinion which tells you what to modify, to change, or to remove. Be open and objective in forming an opinion, and do not be afraid to admit mistakes.

Learning to balance subjectivity and objectivity takes time, but it is not impossible to acquire the skills of critical listening.

Why Listening Is Important To A Music Producer

Just as a writer learns to write by actual writing, if you want to improve as a music producer, you need to produce. Production should be of paramount importance to you. But, there is an element which should be next in importance, and that is, *listening to music.*

You might argue that you are listening to music. You listen to music when you are hanging out with friends or driving your car. This kind of listening is passive listening. As a music producer, what you need is intentional listening. If you don't listen with intent, your progress as a producer will surely be slow and might even stop you from producing great music.

A belief that goes around about listening to music, a producer loses originality and becomes a hindrance in creating unique music. This is far from the truth and is harmful for several reasons.

For one, it is not possible to create an original or unique music since it is inevitable to be influenced by something. Another is that, by listening to music the music that we create ends up unoriginal. The music that you create is not original if you listen to one or two music the whole life.

The reverse is true. Through frequent listening to music, you are building ideas and sounds. These ideas and sound will become your materials in creating something unique. By limiting yourself from listening to music, you are actually stopping your creative potential and from becoming a successful music producer.

Types of Listening

There are two types of listening which should be your foundation in your work as a music producer. One is critical listening and the other is analytical listening. For an aspirant music producer, you need to learn both types and how to apply them to your work. Here, if you are to attain the desired result, you need to be both sound engineer and music producer.

Critical listening
From the sound engineer's point of view, critical listening is what he needs as he listens to the physical details of the music. These physical details include frequencies, tone, imaging, dynamic range, and how instruments blend. This skill allows him control of the technical aspect of music is as it enables him to deal with the issues in music performances and how they integrate. For instance, frequencies in musical performances overlap and prevent each performance from being clearly heard. Or perhaps, the sound of one instrument is not what it should have been and needs processing for it to come out realistically in production.

The technical aspects of production should not be everything. There are productions that are perfect technically, but don't feel great and lifeless and cold. It is also necessary to understand how the physical aspects affect the feeling of the musical performance.

Analytical listening
This type of listening is about meaning and feeling. The sounds we hear in our everyday life convey meaning. Listen to

the way a word sounds and you get a feeling and the meaning of the word. For instance, a hello may sound friendly to one or it could mean being surprised at seeing somebody. The feeling one gets from a word is in the way it is said and conveyed.

The same thing in a musical performance, the emotional intention of the music is in the sound. It is, therefore, necessary that the emotional content of the songs must be brought out. And here, the music producer analyzes the sound so that everything in the production can convey the meaning and intention of the music to the listeners. The meaning out of the song is its essence. Without the essence of the song, the listeners are likely to get confused.

If the sounds do not fuse together in a vocal performance and reinforce the meaning of the song, you miss that which is critically important to a song. Note that no one sound works for every recording type and for every music style. It is the task of the music producer or sound engineer to determine the kind of sound you are after and to bring out its meaning. Decisions derived from analytical listening are not within the parameters of critical analysis.

No two songs are the same. The purpose of analyzing a song for its feeling and meaning is to control the performers, guiding them to perform according to the needs of the song. Also, a producer cannot just use the same techniques for two different kinds of music. For instance, one must not apply the miking technique used for a rock song and also used it in a ballad. The result would not only sound strange but off. Further, a misfit of technique would hamper the musician's ability to interpret the song properly.

How To Listen Critically To Music

Detachment
You may enjoy listening to a particular music because it means something special to you. Because you enjoy listening to it, you find it difficult to detach from the music in order to form an opinion about it. The listening could be doubly difficult for a novice music producer. But, as you gain more experience in creating and producing music, you will learn how to stand outside of that feeling of enjoyment the music generates in you. And, as you remove yourself from emotional attachment, you begin to analyze the music as to its flaws and merits.

You may look at detachment as a kind of switch that you can turn on or off whenever you feel the need for it. Many of the music professions find it difficult to turn the switch on or off. But, acquiring this ability is helpful as it helps you experience two kinds of listening: from the aspect of enjoying the music, and from the aspect of detailed analysis.

Note, however, that the music you listen to may be one which you do not enjoy. This is where detachment and objectivity will be of great aid to you.

Listening
A music producer cannot do away with listening. It is an integral part of his work. But it is not as much as knowing how to listen but how you apply it to the production process. You may hear seasoned music producers claim they know how to listen intently to music and to listen accurately. They might even claim to hear how music should sound even before actually hearing them.

Seasoned producers may have acquired the expertise to listen from long experience in music production. But, for aspiring producers, they have to train in the ways of listening. If you search the web, you will come across several guides on how to listen to music. But, the best way to acquire your listening skill is *to listen*.

If you are new to music production, purchase a pair of trusted monitor speakers, set it up in a conducive environment, and listen to as music as you can. The environment's reflective surfaces should be at its minimum, and position the monitors and yourself in an equilateral triangle. The purpose of having these monitors is to have your ears develop an affinity or relationship with the speakers. Getting used to your monitor speakers gives you the advantage of producing results efficiently and fast wherever you are. The results are made possible by having to listen to the speakers using your reference material, allowing you to focus on each element of the sound.

Listening to the same pair of speakers should have familiarized you with the voicing of the monitors, like how a specific instrument stands out or how vocals elevate from the mix. Being used to your monitors heightens your focus and attention to sound details and facilitates a transparent connection between the music and your ears. As a result, you become more confident in making decisions without the necessity of having to listen as often to your reference material.

Getting the best experience out of listening, the key is the right monitoring environment.

A poor listening equipment and environment might distract your thoughts and decisions when you work. Should you prefer, you can imitate the studio conditions by listening to nearfield monitors. Position your nearfield monitors at the same orientation and height as on a meter bridge and you get the chance of experiencing sound as they should be when in a session. There are producers who carry with them trusted monitor speakers when doing projects. An example is Bob Clearmountain who carried his own computer speakers, and became an award-winning success.

Working With A Reference Material

A reference material is handy when you work in a studio with different monitors, and you do not have your own to work on. It could also be inconvenient to be carrying your equipment from studio to studio when working on your projects. Using a reference point to educate you to the color and tone of the monitors, and the acoustic environment you have to work on.

It is common now for producers to always carry with them a CD of selected genres and well-known tracks. One track may contain acoustic drum sound which can serve as your reference point when mixing or tracking. Or one track may have show the dynamic range and blend of instrumentation. This can be a perfect mix for you and can become your blueprint to the relationship of the different frequencies you expect in the mix. You can then use the blueprint to imitate the relationship of frequencies.

A benefit you get from using a reference material is it gives you the ability to detect the characteristics of the environment and the new monitor. Using your reference material, you can assess the sounds of the different instruments you. The use of the reference material also makes up for your lack of knowledge about the monitor in question.

The Way The Buying Public Listens

New technologies have changed the way the public listens. The buying public today has a wide choice in terms of equipment, modes, and formats. With this as the background, the goal of production is to make sure that music produced is aimed for the equipment it is going to be played.

Today, the MP3 dominates the listening public. This device comes with inexpensive earphones acceptable reproductions. A concern expressed by professionals is that the listener may not hear music in its intended sonic form. Another listening environment which issues concern from professionals is the car, the sound of which can be unpredictable.

As a result, professionals are now similar systems to benchmark their materials. For example, using an iPod for monitoring purposes may be considered wrong by some, but could check if the mixes translate as expected. Headphones is another way of monitoring and may be viewed in a negative or positive way. Headphones as a monitoring system can be negative as units widely vary and most of the listening public no longer listen on them. It is a positive system since with the right headphones, the finer details of the music can be heard.

Chapter 9. The Most Important Skill For Music Producers

It is not an easy task for a music producer to listen to music. It should be noted that there are peculiarities in the ways we listen to music and how our brains interpret the music heard.

Whichever way people listen to music, it is to the advantage of the music producer, especially for the new ones, to know the different ways we listen to music. Knowledge in this can greatly benefit the producer in working through the stages of music production.

The Ways Of Listening

Humans by nature can tune out certain sounds, as evidenced in the cocktail party phenomenon. The cocktail party effect is where the listener is in a crowded room heavy with noise. As expected, the focus of the listener is on the conversation with the person in front. Despite the concentration on the topic, their heads turn by hearing their name called or upon hearing the sound of something that catches the interest of their minds.

The ability to switch focus tells us that we are able to listen and process in a critical way the key aspects of the background noise, such that we are alert to key words or sound that interest us. Music producers and sound engineers use this ability, whether they are aware of it or not. The cocktail party effect can be interpreted in many ways. It, however, suggests that the listeners' mind is alert to everything, whether by intention or otherwise.

Switching focus is a powerful tool, especially in accessing crucial information on a project you are working on, having in mind the discerning buyers. If you can hear your material on different levels, you can understand how your material is perceived by the background radio listener, or by one who sings along the vocals, or by fellow professionals who analyze the song in many ways.

People have peculiarities in the way they listen to music and in how our brains process the information received. Our brain receives information from the sensory organs, and then transforms sensations, like sound waves, heat, touch, and light into electrochemical signals. These signals are, in turn, transformed by brain algorithms for processing. When the information is processed, it passes through an attention filter which determines its importance and which cognition the filtered information should be made available to. This process and recognition is what allows a person to pick out a name despite the noise in a crowded room.

We can analyze the ways we listen to music, but a good place to start is what Bob Katz (2007) in his *Mastering Audio, The Art and The Science* refers to as *active* and *passive* listening. Active listening is the complete focus on listening, regardless if the focus is on an element or elements or the whole piece of music. Passive listening is the background music you listen to while working on something else. Both suggest levels of concentration which a person can have.

Another way of listening is what is referred to as *micro* and *macro* listening. To understand macro listening, think of it as viewing a town from a high altitude. From up high you can appreciate the view of the town's landscape, seen from a distance. In music, macro listening allows the listener to appreciate the whole sound. Macro listening is focused listening on the whole song at the same time, not to any element of the song. This way of listening requires detachment which gives you objectivity when you need it.

Micro is the innate listening ability that enables you to focus on a single aspect of the track. The conversation in our cocktail party is an example for this way of listening. To go back to our town landscape example above, This would be zooming in on a particular street and focus on its surroundings.

The four ways of listening mentioned are valuable for producers and sound engineers and can be honed through experience. Producers and engineers spend years of training to acquire the ability to listen to the details of sound coming in from monitors at the same time. Only a few achieve this ability, and still others find it difficult to switch off.

Holistic listening is another way of listening but broader than macro. The term refers to your appreciation of the program music, or the whole album, viewing it as something small and tangible. You can compare this to the process of listening used by a mastering engineer working on a project. The engineer might be doing macro listening when working on an individual track, but is also concerned with the holistic.

The holistic way of listening is a skill imperative for the producer especially when assessing the overall sound of the album or project. The assessment done through holistic manner succeeds when the sonic objectives of the project are achieved. Holistic way of listening is, therefore, a necessary skill a producer should develop.

To develop switching of listening focus, following these steps and do it as an exercise:

- Place a busy track with large amount of instrumentation on your monitoring environment
- Try to identify the instrumentation you hear and do switching of focus starting with your normal listening level
- Focus on one instrument
- Zoom out and listen to as much music as possible
- Try listening at the holistic level, being high above and listening with detachment
- Assess intensities and frequencies in aspects of the sound.

Going micro
When you have gone through the holistic way of listening, it is time to zoom in on a particular. At this point is, you might ask: Once you are in "a particular" aspect of the sound, what do you do? What are you listening for?

With micro listening, you could listen to an instrument on your mixing console, But, once there, how do you assess the sound of the instrument? What are you looking for? Is it the sound, the timbre, the capture, the frequency range, or the performance?

At the micro level, what you are concerned with is the smallest aspect of the performance in terms of timing, tuning, and delivery. At this level, you can be analytical as you listen to a solo track, focused on each aspect of the sound with each pass.

If you do micro listening this way, it will be easy for you to do your analysis. Separating the same instrument presented to you while immersed in listening to the whole track is a skill which could be difficult, but can be developed. When this skill is developed, you will discover that it is an invaluable skill for a producer to possess.

To make an assessment of sound, you can have your own listening analysis framework which will serve as your guide in making educated assessment of sound parameters.

A listening framework serves as your starting point, breaking down a recording and evaluating how it actually sounds. In this framework, you listen through several passes. Passes mean the number of times the tape is played back.

In the *first pass*, the thing assessed is the form of drums, analyzing its rhythmical elements. This analysis reveals the time signature and provides insights into the sound's groove. If you take a step further and link the bass of the piece, you can determine the construction of the song. You can determine if syncopation is present and what the bass is playing. You can expand this pass further.

In the *second pass*, your attention shifts to the more musical aspect of the piece. The concern here is the chord structure, arrangement, and backing or the music's construction. It is at this point that you identify the main feeder. The main feeder is that instrument that is the driving force of the song, the element in the song that makes it memorable. An example of this instrument is the pounding of the piano chords.

In the *third pass*, the sound quality is assessed and dissected for its construction. It is in this pass that you go into the macro and micro listening. Macro listening is where you assess the balance of the instrument, and the micro is where you focus on each element in the mix and their sonic quality.

Once you get the overview of your listening framework, you can scribble comments, according to each area in the framework.

Chapter 10. Being a Music Producer

The concept of a music producer has changed over time and the work involved has also evolved. The producer role of George Martin, considered as the role model of the 1900s, is now considered as traditional. The creative role exemplified by Martin and described in Chapter 2 of this book is no longer enough to make it in the digital landscape of today's music industry.

The workload of the music producer now not only includes the creative side of production, but also the technical and the business side of producing music. The producer has to make decisions on the fly, be able to communicate the meaning of the song to all involved, like the audio engineers, the singer, and the musicians. The works of the producer encompass a wide range of responsibilities in the whole production process.

These responsibilities call for the music producer to be equipped with knowledge, skills and attributes to be able to manage and supervise artists, the people involved in the whole production process, the budgeting and financing, and the marketing of the product.

What a music producer needs

Communication skills
Producers deal with different people all throughout the production process. Not only must the producer deal with people directly involved in production, but must also connect with people for the business aspect of production. After all, the finished product needs to be sold, distributed, and advertised.

Music producers, therefore, should be good communicators. They need to know their artists, consider their views to gain their trust and work with the producer in experimenting sounds. This ability requires knowing how to listen, being diplomatic, and communicating clearly. Listening means doing so with empathy and attention to elicit understanding.

Relationships with artists have to be managed on different levels. You will be working long sessions in a recording studio which is a close environment. Long sessions can become tedious, in which case, you need to use a blend of skills to keep the session flow smoothly. You might find yourself taking on the role of a friend, a counselor, a colleague, and in some cases, a psychiatrist.

Imagine a scenario where a musician bares their emotions in a song about love lost or the loss of a loved one. Recalling the loss of a loved one can leave them exposed and emotional. This can lead to a loss of confidence. As the person responsible for the recording session, it is necessary that you keep the artist in a productive frame of mind.

Uncontrolled outbursts of artists' emotions can get in the way of the recording session. How you negotiate the situation through communication is the key to move the project forward. Also, your style of communicating will help you get along with the artists. Each artist will have different characteristics, and therefore, you need to adapt your communication style for different artists and in different situations. If you are familiar with the vocabulary of the studio and know something about the genre, these will aid you in translating your ideas to the artist.

If you are successful in communicating with your artists, they might discuss the background of their life and their music. These are valuable information which can help you in shaping your music.

Composure
Working in a creative industry is fun. It can also be difficult, especially when you are constrained by time and budget. Working under pressure can affect you, your work, and the people around you. It is during such times that you need to compose yourself. Without composure, it is easy for conflict to arise in tight situations and break relationships.

Composure is self-control. It is how you manage your emotions, have empathy with the emotions of others, and how you manage your response. Self-control is necessary because how you carry yourself speaks much to others.

Body Language
It is not only words that communicate, so does your body. Your body language is a medium of communication which conveys messages across, just as you receive messages from the body language of the artists around you. As a producer, you have to be careful with the body language you provide, making sure that you convey positive signals. At the same time, you have to be alert to the body language of the people you are working with.

Often, body language speaks more than words. Therefore, by understanding the body language your artists, you can tell what they are trying to say and allow you to develop an appropriate plan of action. Imagine a scenario where the spoken words do not synchronize with the body language. For instance, a vocalist who happens to be the songwriter does not agree with how the guitar is played. The vocalist may say "Fine, let Freddie play what he wants", but it is said with a slouched shoulders and disapproving eyes.

There are many ways to resolve the situation. One is, you choose diplomacy and work out for a simple guitar solo that fits the song or go for multiple guitar tracks. At the same time, you have to control your that your body language sends encouraging signals.

Attire

What you wear helps you communicate the image you want to project. You may dress in a flamboyant way, or you may want an attire that makes you look confident and sure of yourself. Since you will be working for long sessions, you may opt to wear comfortable clothes or com in your particular style.

A music producer must understand the importance of attire, since the choice of dress affects your self-image, the impression that you want others to see, and the way people you work with behave towards you.

Confidence

It is often necessary for music producers to make split-second decisions and have the last say in making music. You cannot, therefore, waver when confronted with difficult situations. When making such decisions, you are confident that you are doing the right thing. Hesitate and the people around you will lose confidence in you.

Confidence is an ability which is learned and developed over time. You may not have much confidence when new to music production, but as you become familiar with everything about music production, you would have the confidence to succeed and be proud of your work.

Confidence is belief in your abilities and capabilities. To be confident is to be realistic of what you can do, and to feel secure in that knowledge. Be careful not to have too much confidence so as not to look arrogant and cocky. It is also not desirable to have little confidence as this will prevent you from making quick decisions, prevent you from experimenting with sounds, and cause you to miss opportunities.

There are two kinds of confidence: the inner and the external confidence. *Your inner confidence* is what gives you strength and resiliency when faced with changes and challenges. Inner confidence comes from skills you developed out of your working experience in the music industry. These could be skills in music, audio engineering, music production, mixing, and the other skills required in the process of making music.There are, therefore, your core skills.

Your inner skill manifests through your external confidence. Therefore, it is necessary to develop your inner confidence first before you tackle the external confidence. *External confidence* is your ability to accept how people see you – both positive and negative perception - and to embrace them. When you are able to accept others' views, then you can say that you have a solid foundation of internal confidence.

For the music producer, the confidence that you show can remove the fears within your musicians, allow for ideas to flow, and develop trust in the vision for their music, and the guidance you provide. The musicians know what they want. But they lose sight of what they want as they focus on perfecting their instruments and their parts. This is where trust in your guidance matters.

Attitude

Attitude is how we respond to people, things, placed, and events in our life. In the music production environment, attitude can make or break the music or the project. Attitude is crucial in the workplace as this determines the choices you or the musicians make.

Many producers expect the people they work with, whether they be musicians, engineers, or assistant, to have a "can do" attitude, to be responsive, and have the vision of what the music is going to be. They want their musicians to be able to pick up cues from other members of the team, allowing the production process to move forward smoothly.

Bringing out the positive attitude from musicians and engineers, however, require good communication skill from the music producer. The producer must understand that attitude is not fixed but can change when confronted with different situations and experiences. What the producer must do is to provide the right environment and atmosphere to elicit the positive attitude from team members.

Networking

We have to admit it, success is not always because of what you know but who you know. Especially in the music industry, reputation matters. The question is: How do we get to know those we should know? And, how do we achieve that reputation and be considered a music producer of note? The answer is through *networking*.

It is a natural tendency of people who like each other to work together. Like, it is useless to go on a long tour when you don't get along well with the vocalist or lead guitarist. The tour bus becomes your mobile prison. On the other hand, when people who get along well work together, the work could be fun. Working together involves trust. For instance, if you trust and see someone as reliable, you are more inclined to give the work to that person.

Why network?

The music industry is a people business. To get into the music business, you need to expand your contacts, and this is where networking can help you. You can meet people in the music community by joining associations and organizations associated with music, like music guilds for one.

Networking is building relationships – we form new relationships and strengthen the old ones. Another way of looking at networking is communicating. Communicating may be face-to-face, over the phone, and until recently, through computers and mobile devices. It may be easy nowadays to communicate through gadgets, but nothing beats face-to-face communication. With interpersonal communication, you get to see facial expressions, eye contact, and interpreting body language. The information you get out of this kind of communication is far richer than one you get from computers or the web.

You can expand your circle of contacts and start to build relationships by attending gigs and events. Meet people and get them to like you, develop affinity and rapport. And, more importantly, build trust that would make the relationship last long, become meaningful and sustainable.

The key to building relationship is having the right attitude. The reason many fear networking is because they feel ineffective in communicating the right way and in an ethical manner. Poor communication skills, which include listening, and the absence of ethical standards can result to rude and discourteous behaviors. If people read you as not useful to them, they ignore you or leave your side.

So, why go out and meet people? You do so to:
- Enhance your profile
- Know your marketplace
- Get valuable information you can use
- Meet people you can work with in the future
- Meet reputable people and decision makers in the music industry
- Gain knowledge of what other people in the music industry do
- Let other people know what you do
- Help others with musical difficulties and challenges

If you are new to music production and to networking, it is natural to have some reservations. However, it's something you have to deal with because it can have such a significant impact on your career.

Chapter 11. Bringing Clarity To Music

We have today millions of songs readily available through mobile devices, thanks to the advancing technology. We can access more music than it was possible before, and still more music is being produced. It is understandable that there will be more diversity in the kind of music that we are exposed to, with boundaries that separate genres getting blurred than previously experienced.

When organizing your music library or buying CDs, the first thing you look is the music genre. Genre is how we navigate through music of our choice. On a socio-cultural level, it is how artists forms their public identities, it shows how the music industry organizes itself, how band members meet, venues book band, producers choose artists and music, what radio stations choose music to play, and how listeners look for music to enjoy.

There may be those who claim that the use of genre is on the decline. The fact is, labeling has been in use for the past century and is still in use today.

The Importance of Genre

Classification of music into genres has been a subject of debate among music scholars and those involved in the music industry. There are those who say that using genres to identify a song is elitist and unnecessary. Others claim that genres restrict the artists' creativity and reduce people's enjoyment of the music.

On the positive side, there are musicians who argue that classifying music makes it easy to see patterns and helps listeners find creations that satisfy individual tastes. Still others argue that genres enhance listening pleasures, and provide opportunities to honor and recognize the artists' creative decisions in making music, especially those who experiment with new styles.

When done improperly, classifying music may mislead the listener, and instances of misuse have been observed. Further, wrong classification of music may not express the subtle experience of listening. These arguments, however, are not enough to dismiss genres, since the benefits outweigh the problems caused by wrongful applications. When done properly, genres enhance the clarity of the music, and the recognition hardworking artists deserve.

1. Clarity

It is our nature to make sense of the world and our experiences, and this includes our music listening experiences. At its core, this is the reason for classifying music. It gives us the means to perceive what we hear accurately and share them to others. Genres allow us to talk about music, of relationships between songs, albums, artists, and time periods.

Classifying music evaluates the unique characteristics of each song and album and locates them in categories close to related creations. The genre's boundaries are marked by the sparseness or density of common traits. Heavy clusters of similar creations form the core of a music style, while the relative gaps or distinctive differences are the demarcation lines.

An aspect of classification is that it changes over time as new knowledge about creations and the relatives emerge. An instance is where artists produce new styles of music. This aspect makes new genres flexible and loose. They get to be established when hundreds and more albums are produce in and around it.

But, there will always be gray areas that blur the demarcation lines and songs may overlap between categories. Classifications of music are approximations and are relative, which means, no final or "correct" categorization.

Not all creations can be described with a single label. For purposes of clarity, labeling often use multiple genre names, blend words, and add adjectives. Few examples are traditional heavy metal, death-thrash, and cybersynth. Fundamentally, genre names are reflexive way of recognizing and describing music; it is not a hard-line system of boundaries.

2. Recognition

An assumption goes around that classifying music into genres restricts the artists' creativity or limits their creative freedom. People see genres as a box where new music is placed and described with unnecessary labels. It is not to be denied that classification can be done to the extreme and become an absurdity. But, this does not negate the value of a properly done classification. Labels that are properly done are relevant and meaningful and tend to stick while the frivolous labels are easily forgotten.

It is recommended for fans, music journalists, and artists to constantly adapt the genre's language to stay abreast with music innovations. Rather than worry over restrictions and generalizations, people should be open-minded when encountering new terms, and people should be willing to create them. The creation of new genre labels is necessary and an ongoing process; this is showing respect to artistic exploration.

The claim that genre classification is elitist and that one music is superior over another is not true. Admittedly, each person has personal tastes and preferences in music, but no one should make a claim that a style of music is better than another. This is not what genre classifications means and what it is for.

For instance, to say that Slipknot is not a metal band is not meant to be an offense to the group. It is a way of recognizing that the ideas and creativity of the band's music distinguishes them from that of the metal band. In terms of recognition and clarity, the new creation deserves to be recognized with a new descriptors and language that is descriptive of the level of creativity of the group.

 3. Appreciation

Appreciation is the greatest reason for assigning music to a genre. Doing so offers listeners enhanced appreciation and enjoyment on a personal level. A deep and broad understanding of the genre results from identifying specific artistic choices and associates them to related creations. Understanding then makes it easier to detect innovation and the level of skill of the songwriter. Without the connections, the song and the album exist in a conceptual vacuum without context. In this condition, it is difficult to appreciate music in its finer points, not to mention its innovations.

One way to enhance the enjoyment of music is to listen to as many songs as possible and compare the strengths and weaknesses of each song in relation to one another. Take for instance a professional wine steward who has tasted hundreds and more of wine and yet can distinguish differences and similarities in each wine. It is the same with music. The music lover can then share with others these similarities and differences and make suggestions.

Genre names, therefore, are important means of describing music and an essential component in experiencing music. Appreciation of music is enhanced when discussed with others.

4. Understanding the listeners

Understanding the genre is crucial to understanding the listeners. Genres reflect a culture. That is to say, fans of a genre or a sub-genre gather in the same venues, same shops, listen to the same kind of music, same radio stations, same movies, and visit the same websites.

These information are valuable in promoting and marketing music or in organizing live shows. If you are an artist, understanding genres will help you reach your target listeners and increase your chances of success. It can also give you ideas for your design of your cover art and product.

5. Decision-making

Knowing the genre helps musicians choose the right label to use for their music creation or decide whether they need a label. For example, pop music can have the advantage of using a label for their music, while indie rock can make do with an indie imprint, which can be released easier.

Defining genres

Music genre is a system or a tool used to classify pieces of music as belonging to a set of conventions or shared tradition.

They are categories which emerged through a complex interaction of artists, culture, and market forces with the purpose of identifying similarities (and differences) in music creations, and to organize the collection of music.

Music is grouped into five and a rich history is behind each group. These groups are: Folk Music, Classical Music, World Music, Utility Music, and Popular Music. Popular music is the largest of the groups. One should bear in mind that music is a dynamic phenomenon – it is always changing, evolving, and transforming like a giant organism. No music genre just suddenly appears and become revolutionary without having an origin. Each music evolved, merged, mutated, or have become extinct.

A type of music may have emerged as a result of concentrations of artists with many similar traits, creating new songs with distinctive and unique sounds, and eventually forming into a genre. But, what defines the genre is more than sounds and the technical aspects. It is also defined by subculture, geography, fashion, period of time, and mentality. One can therefore look at music genres as a concentration in network nodes or musical networks having a large group of music connected by technique, instrumentation, ideology or mentality, place, time, and sound.

How a genre gets its name happen in different ways. A music journalist may have given a name to a group of similar music to summarize concealed events in the past. Another possibility is the mixing of records from different genres. When a community accepts these mixes, new records are produced to approximate the combinations and a new genre is born.

The amount of genres today is overwhelming. Some of these genres are subgenres of a larger genre or closely associated to another. The birth of a new genre is always a possibility, or the recreation of a past genre with small alteration, what is known as a *revival*. In the past 2 decades, revivals have become part of popular music.

The evolution of popular music genres

As mentioned above, the world of music is divided into five groups, the largest of which is popular music. Popular music traces its influences from the other worlds forming super-genres: Industrial and Gothic, Heavy Metal, Rock N' Roll, Pop Music, Country, Rhythm N' Blues, Blues, Jazz, Jamaican, RAP, Electronic Dance Music (EDM)-Breakbeat, EDM- Drum N' Bass, EDM-Hardcore, EDM-Techno, EDM House, EDM-Trance, and Downtempo.

Industrial and Gothic

This genre lies between electronic music and rock. It came out of the underground scene during the German Post-war (1970s). Gothic music, which followed the "Post-Dunk Depression", exhibits similar characteristics with Industrial and both became meshed.

Industrial derived its name from Industrial Records, the first industrial record at the time which was more an experiment than a real commercial enterprise. Musical creations made references to factory and industry, such as machines and noise, which served to strengthen the genre's name. Industrial's music leans towards anti-music (noise) and synth to create the feel of retro-futurism or techno-paranoia. Industrial borrowed the structure of Rock songs and the instrumentation of electronic music, like Downtempo, Trance, and Techno. Adapting Techno, this led to industrial genres, like *Dark Techno, Techno, Cybertechno*, to mention a few.

Sub-genres:
- Krautrock
- Avant Garde Industrial
- Noise Music
- Electronic Body Music
- Darkwave and Coldwave
- Dark Ambient
- Synth and Minimal Industrial (Revival)

Heavy Metal

From its name, people would mistake this super-genre as a faster type of Rock. The fact is, Heavy Metal grew out of *The Devil's Music* - Blues. In the seventies, Metal's experimental phase, it was then referred to as Classic Metal. But it divested the blues influence and evolved into different styles and retained two elements: one was the text about nihilism, sorrow, and pain; the other was the hidden subtext which revolved around the Devil, representing destruction, death, black, corpses, and evil themes.

The name *Heavy Metal* is descriptive of its two aspects: it has more amplification and distortion than rock, and it is too metallic, which means too technical and rational.It has distinctive elements which are highly technical, such as double bass drums, blast beats, lightning guitar solos, 12 string bass, voice techniques that are difficult, like screeching and grunting. Riff is an important element in Heavy Metal music and forms its foundation of many of their songs. The early Metal compositions with riffs use the triton, an interval of three whole tones which sound dissonant and conveys a feeling of restlessness.

Heavy Metal's origin can be traced to Steppenwolf's "Born to be Wild" which included the line "Heavy Metal Thunder". This super-genre is popular among the nerds, which is understandable since the music is for the analytical mind. It has become a highly examined super-genre with over 50 sub-genres.

Sub-genres:
Classic Metal
Power Metal
Extreme Metal (Black and Speed)
Grindcore
Symphonic Metal and Gothic Metal
Metal Core

Rock N' Roll

In the fifties, Rock N' Roll was in its infancy. Rock's primitive form were Skiffle, Folk Revivals, and Rockability which points to a slow development before it reached the Golden Age of Rock. Rock N' Roll – the main genre - is considered as a groundbreaking milestone in music and succeeded in breaking social barriers. It also was able to break the barrier between the adults and the young.

Rock N' Roll lost its bold spirit and the craze went down slope in the sixties. The music became politically correct and well-behaved and Soul became the dominant force in music. It was when the "Twist" – swinging and shaking dance – became popular that Rock was revived and was prevented from becoming totally extinct.

Rock N' Roll gradually faded in the following decades. But, interest in earlier subcultures in the thirties (dance and music) and the Rock N' Roll in the fifties shows that this super-genre can still excite the youth. This is understandable since Rock N' Roll music is about energy and tempo. It pulls people to lose themselves and become wild.

Sub-genres:
Skiffle (Revival)
Surf Rock
Rockabilly
Garage Rock
British and American Folk Revival

Golden Age/Classic Rock

Rock exploded in indescribable way in the sixties, so much so that many music journalists considered it as the most influential popular music genre. Music magazines, books, festivals use the term "Rock" as the case for all popular music. You will find artists who still perform "Rock" to this very day, a justification and proof for the term "Golden Age".

The context of the Classic Rock's revolution was during the long period of prosperity which followed World War II. A belief in the better future became the blueprint the counterculture hippie movement. Amphetamine, which was used during the war, became cheaper and more popular. The amphetamine shaped the energetic music during this time, while the psychedelic drug paved the way for experimentation and genre differentiation.

Classic Rock assimilated the elements from R&B and Blues and Rock took hold. Classic Rock became more structured, like the sequential pattern verse, chorus, verse, chorus, break/solo, and chorus. The opposite is true with Prog Rock and experimental acid Rock which has no structure.

With Rock's Golden Age, the multi-tracking recording studios emerged. Multi-tracking gave the artists freedom to record different song parts and to edit separately. Many techniques also became possible: cutting, time alteration, leslie speakers, echo, and more. The pioneering techniques during the Classic Rock Era paved the way for music that could not be performed live and were produced as music albums.

The sounds created during this time were out-of-this-world and intriguing; they were experimental sounds which further contributed to the Rock mania. This was the time of famous producers George Martin, Phil Spector, and Brian Wilson.

Sub-genres:
Beat/British Invasion
British Blues and Blues Rock
Folk Rock
Hard Rock
Psychedelic/ Acid Rock
Glam Rock / Shock Rock

Punk Rock/New Wave

Punk, Post-Punk, and the New Wave super-genres achieved evolution in a short span of time. This super-genre started as the purest form of Rock and evolved into a movement that embraced eccentricity. At its early stage, Punk was the opposite of what the New Wave would later become: eclecticism, mass-appeal, heavy post-production, interest from adults, and stardom. Rock had then lost its connection with the youth crowd.

Punk origins go way before the seventies. Its idea of short, energetic songs and power riffs comes from the Power Pop. The power chords formed as the basis for punk sons. The early Punk bands were amateurish that the name became synonymous with ineptitude; anyone can do Punk music, regardless of music background. Punk music attracted the youth who were spontaneous, raw, lo-fi, and sincere.

On the technical side, Punk was characterized with inadequate instrumentation. Chords used were simple though powerful, and the vocals had narrow dynamic range. The days of Punk and New Wave had strong influences new technology, forceful imagery, and shocking personalities. Their focus were more on message and concept pessimism, being cynical, melancholic, and undermining.

Sub-genres:
Punk Rock
Anarcho-Punk and crust punk
Pub rock and Proto punk
No wave
Horror punk and psychobilly

Alternative Rock / Indie

This genre became a phenomenon during the 70s and dominated Rock in that decade. Alternative rock is a cluster of different styles from the mid-80s to the millennium. But, compared to rock genres at that time, it displays more common ground. Alternative rock is known by distortion on pedals and amps, jangly guitars, dark or sentimental lyrics, and hints of syth.

The name Indie in Indie rock is short for "independent." Indies are smaller and not much oriented on profits. They were intended choice by new artists or taken as the only resort by amateur bands. These new musicians were passionate about their music despite whims of big producers. Or, they may have failed to get into the mainstream.

Alternative rock is much underestimated, especially against the backdrop of the booming EDM. The reason for its persistence is its ability to connect to the youth's soul at the time: frustrations, doubts, anger, depression and fear. This genre still popular, but this could be because it has become a convenient label for what is raw, heavy rock band in music that is not easy to categorize. And, many bands were tagged as alternative though they not truly are. It was just a cool name attached to rock, and used as a good marketing device.

Sub-genres:
Jangle Pop / Indie Rock
Grunge
Dream pop and Shoegaze
Noise rock
Alternative Rock/ Indie II
Rap rock, Funk metal, and Rap core

Contemporary Rock

Contemporary Rock represents the new rock genres of the 21st century. They share common characteristics, though not necessarily technical ones. The rise of these 21st rock genres are shaped by recycling and eclecticism. The take techniques from the old genres and use them to form new ones. They focus on sound quality of music and look for their personal sound. One can describe the genres in the 21st century as a "fusion".

The contemporary rock's power lies in its reaching out to other music genres, leading to the demise of sub-cultural niches. An example of this genre is "Mash-up" which merges all types of genres to become an eclectic mix – a mashing of styles that are unrelated.

Between 1999 to 2002, Dance music grew popular than Rock, which threatened the Rock enthusiasts. But, at the beginning of the millennium Contemporary Rock remained powerful, pushing Dance Music to the back. Today, Contemporary Rock remains a powerful music genre. With the emergence of websites and streaming apps, we perhaps see a hint of a future with no genre monopoly.

Sub-genres:
Emo-rock
Garage and post-punk revivals
Dance-punk and Nu-rave
Post-Britpop
New Prog/Post Prog

Pop Music

The Pop Music genre owes its existence from Rock music (60s to 80s), but this shifted towards House and R&B in the 90s. Pop music is characterized by:

- pronounced melodies,
- radio friendly or music which was edited to play up to four minutes
- politically correct music

- easy song structures
- easy chords
- easy to memorize
- strong emphasis on video performance and video clips
- has a commercial nature, or creates what sells most

Pop music's strength in its denial of a niche; it includes anyone who wants to have fun in music. What defines pop music is whatever that appeals most to the public. And, what appeals most to the people becomes the core between varying musical tastes. It is also the most flexible and applicable of any and all styles.

Sub-genres:
Skiffle (revival)
Bubblegum and Teenybop
Country pop and country rock
Singer/songwriter
Synthpop and New Romantics
Indie Pop
Discopop and Post disco
Electroclash

Country music

By its name, Country Music seems to be an insignificant genre. But, Country Music is the most selling genre in decades, especially in the United States, and still is. This genre has always been associated with the radio, and one of the pioneer music genre to be on airwaves.

The subject of country music is diverse, though essentially, it is about family, home, and everyday living. Other subjects of this genre are drugs, liquor, criminal behavior, and adultery which dispel the illusion of a perfect picture. This disillusion became this genre's catalyst to create diversity within the genre.

As an old music genre, Country music is performed with classic string instrument, like the banjo, acoustic guitar, fiddle, harmonica, and violin. Country music has refrained from using other instruments, especially the electronics.

Country often features a slow tempo with emphasis on voice. The voice should be able to convey emotional ballads or stories. It is also common to hear duets in Country music, especially man and woman who sings about love. Country music is based on traditional tunes and ballads, in contrast to plain chords and melodies. It is more akin to folk music.

Country music origins traces back to the remote, rural areas, though it has penetrated the urban landscape. It has a strong link with American culture, giving it a domestic appeal and a weak foreign appeal. However, there are songs and artists that are popular overseas, which proves that the power and emotion of this genre can be transferred in other genres.

Sub-genres:
Western swing
Hillbilly / Classic Country
Bluegrass
Nashville / Countrypolitan
Contemporary Country / Neotraditionalists

Rhythm N' Blues (R&B)

Two old music genres combine to form the Rhythm N' Blues super-genre. One is the rhythm of the Gospel which provides a groovy tempo already evident with handclapping and rhythmical vibrating voices. The other is the Blues which provides rich bass and warm chords. The two – Gospel and Blues – combines to form different musical elements which made it highly flexible and a hybrid genre.

It also served as a bridge to many super-genres. It is considered as the interface between Blues and Rock, Gospel and House, and Rap and Pop and is therefore the most accessible of the music genres.

The essential aspect of R&B is its backbeat. That is, an accent marks the 2nd and 4th beat of each line, making a cadence. R&B is danceable music, mainly due to the backbeat. This rhythm gradually evolved into Disco music, clubbing, and the nightlife culture. R&B is known for its rhythms and drums, and is also responsible for the introduction of breakbeat with strong emphasis on percussion.

R&B common subject are joy, love, and optimism which can be heard in most its music. Joy is a trajectory from Blues which found its way in R&B. R&B can be divided into three sub-genres which are equally popular: Soul, Urban, and Funk.

Sub-genres:
Early rhythm and blues
Early Funk & P-Funk
Doo Wop
Soul Blues
Deep Funk / Rare Groove / Nu Funk
Boogie / ElectroFunk

Blues

Blues is as old as popular music and has rich streams from different music genres. Early in its history, it was linked with vice – a song of criminals and outlaws. But, it is better described as the outcry from those in the periphery – the poor and the unfortunates, especially the black. Before R&B, Blues was unfortunately viewed as "race music".

Blues musicians freely travel and perform anywhere, alone or with company, pursuing happiness. A single guitar characterized blues initially but was later accompanied by bass and drums. Its song structure is AAB rhyme performed in harmonic sequences, with a 4/4 rhythm and in 12 bars long.

What is observable in Blues music is its chord progression, which seems to be in a call and response style. The chords are structured with blue notes, that is, notes with pitches that are altered. These chords give blues music sound melancholic and mournful. For black musicians, these connotations did not exist for them.

The degree of Blues as a genre contributed to some structural polarization: modern against classic, acoustic vs electric, and rural against urban. The release of 78rpm Blues records into 33 rpm LPs revitalized the interest in early acoustic Blues in the 60s. This was expanded later by the Acoustic Folk Rock. Unfortunately, Blues was pushed aside by R&B and Rock.

Sub-genres:
Country Blues / Folk Blues
Piano Blues
Texas Blues (Electric)
Chicago Blues / Urban Blues / City Blues
Soul Blues

Jazz

Jazz is played by a group of players, with each player proficient in their own instrument. The instruments used in jazz are saxophones, trumpets, trombones, piano, and string-bass. It is the interaction of these instruments that is crucial to jazz music. The players follow no scores, they feel what the other players in the band play and how their music will evolve. Improvisation and experimentation characterizes Blues music.

Jazz is a combination of African American folk music of the lower class and European amusement and classic music of the upper class. Because of this combination, Jazz is not labeled as Blues. It is, however, noteworthy for binding the subcultures mentioned. The Jazz band is divided into 3 sections: the rhythm played by the piano, drums, and bass provide the beat throughout the track, the melody section performed by the horns is played for the chorus, which is later separated by the solos.

The strength of the Jazz music is in its powerful contrast: chaos vs control, predetermination vs improvisation, sharp and shrill tones against gentle sounds. Jazz is unique in terms of influencing other music genres in subtle ways. Its distinctive instrumentation and concepts are versatile that makes it easy to transfer other popular music genres. Jazz music is divided into three periods: Classic Jazz, Post-Jazz, and Modern Jazz.

Sub-genres:
New Orleans Jazz and Dixieland Jazz
Swing
Chicago Jazz
Bebop
Fusion / Jazz Rock
Acid Jazz / Dance Jazz
Electro Swing

Jamaican Music/Reggae

Jamaican Music was diminished by the more popular Reggae. Reggae's appeal went beyond the threshold used to define world music. But, there are many Jamaican music that grew to be more popular than world music. What is more crucial in Jamaican music is that it creates a shackle between Rap, Dance, and Rock.

Song under the super-genre of Jamaican music share similar characteristics which gives them a distinguishable sound and explains their influence on other music genres., especially the British music. This was so because Jamaica was a British colony up to 1962.

During its time, Jamaica had no radio stations and music televisions and how they enjoy music was through attending local sound systems. These sound systems were mobile and large stereo systems with various types of turntables and speakers. Records were supplied by recording studios which were found everywhere. Because of these recording studios, Jamaican music is not into live performance. Live gigs were non-existent while vinyl was dominant. It is no surprise that many loudspeaker and recording techniques were invented in Jamaica.

A characteristic feature of Jamaican Music is its emphasis on the offbeat. This characteristic gives off a feeling of laidback sound which is good for warm outdoor climate. Other than the technical elements that describe Jamaican music, there are other elements which grew to be a custom overseas, leading to Jamaican or Reggae subgenres.

Sub-genres:
Mento
Rocksteady
Reggae
Dub
2-tone SKA revival, SKA Punk, and SKA Core
Reggae Fusion

Rap and Hip-Hop Music

The Hip-hop contains four elements: breakdancing, turntablism, graffiti, and rapping. Hip-hop, therefore, is not strictly a genre but a wide subculture that encompasses more than music. Rap and Hip-Hop music has two essential elements that define them – the rhyme and the beat.

The word rap is derived from a hip-hop slang which means "flow" (of words).Hip-hops origins is vague and goes way back into the black culture. The word was coined by the Sugar Hill Gang and the Afrika Bambataa which describes a movement, a gathering, or a place of coolness and fun.

The strength of rap lies in its ability convey its message, perhaps due to the use of continuous words all throughout the music. Rap inherited the concepts of sound systems, toasting from Jamaica, and the DJs with turntables.

Sub-genres:
Electro
Golden Age Rap
Jazz Rap / Native Tongue
Reggaeton and Latin Rap
Glitch Hop and Wonky

Breakbeat

The Breakbeat super-genre is defined by its technical components, mainly by its rhythm. There is, however, a racial aspect to this super-genre. Where Rap music is to black, Breakbeat is the Caucasian version. Rap music has an overwhelming number of black artists, whereas Breakbeat has an overwhelming number of white artists. This stirred the Black Dance music genre which led to the emergence of the Jungle.

Breakbeat is part hip-hop with elements of Funk records. It thrives on the samplings taken from Funk records for its breakbeats with elements like turntablism and brekdancing.

The word "breakbeat" comes from the early Funk records where instruments break or stops playing and only the percussion and the drummer remains, referred to as "breakdown." This breakdown section are used by Breakbeat and Rap artists to come up with their own samples without the use of a real drummer and the computer drums. The center between the Drum N' Bass and the Breakbeat are variants of music genres that can, in themselves, be considered as super-genres, like the UK Garage.

Genres
Freestyle and Breakdance
Trip Hop
Electro
Broken Beats
Breakbeat Garage and Grime
EDM Trap / Trapstep

Conclusion

Music has come so far for the last thirty years, evolving at such a high speed. The way people listen to music, how music is produced, and how it is distributed have changed over the years.

For more than fifty years, music industry operated on simple models of making music, and only those with serious resources and years of study and experience in music composition can achieve success.

The crucial moment of transformation in music production was the evolution from analog to digital audio. An even critical transformation occurred in the 90s when the storage system for audio changed from analog audio (cassette tapes and vinyl) to digital storage (CD, Blu-Ray, flash drives).

The music industry landscape may have changed, but still, the future looks interesting for all those involved in music. The mode of business has shifted from the dominant label to a more do-it-yourself culture. Music producers are motivated to look and develop new artists, often using their own resources and succeed.

With the advanced technology that is easily accessible, producers are able to develop new working practices and efficiency measures. Producers can now work creatively and be productive at home, having greater time value and the dedication to get things right with high quality.

What the future offers you are new ways of working for a new musical world. To succeed, however, in this world of music needs dedication, inspiration, passion, and even painstaking hard work.

I hope this book was able to help you to start your career as a music producer. Or, if you are already an expert in this field, this book has given you fresh insights and lead you further exploration and experimentation with sounds.

The next step is to transform what you have learned into actual work and let the experience be a continuing learning process that would direct you to your vision as a proficient music producer.

If you enjoyed this book and found some benefit in reading this, I'd like to hear from you and hope that you could take some time to post a review.

Your feedback and support will help me to greatly improve for future projects and make this book even better.

Thank you and good luck!

Tommy Swindali

www.swindali.com

Discover How To Find Your Sound

Find Out More

Swindali music coaching/Skype lessons.

Email djswindali@gmail.com for info and pricing.

Made in the USA
Coppell, TX
02 December 2019

Download the Audio Book Version of This Book FREE

If you love listening to audio books on-the-go, I have great news for you. You can download the audio book version of this book for FREE just by signing up for a FREE 30-day audible trial! See below for more details!

Audible trial benefits

As an audible customer, you'll receive the below benefits with you 30-day free trial:

- Free audible copy of this book
- After the trial, you will get 1 credit each month to use on any audiobook
- Your credits automatically roll over to the next month if you don't use them
- Choose from Audible's 200,000 titles
- Listen anywhere with the audible app across multiple devices
- Make easy, no hassle exchanges of any audiobook you don't love
- Keep your audiobooks forever, even if you cancel you membership
- and much more...